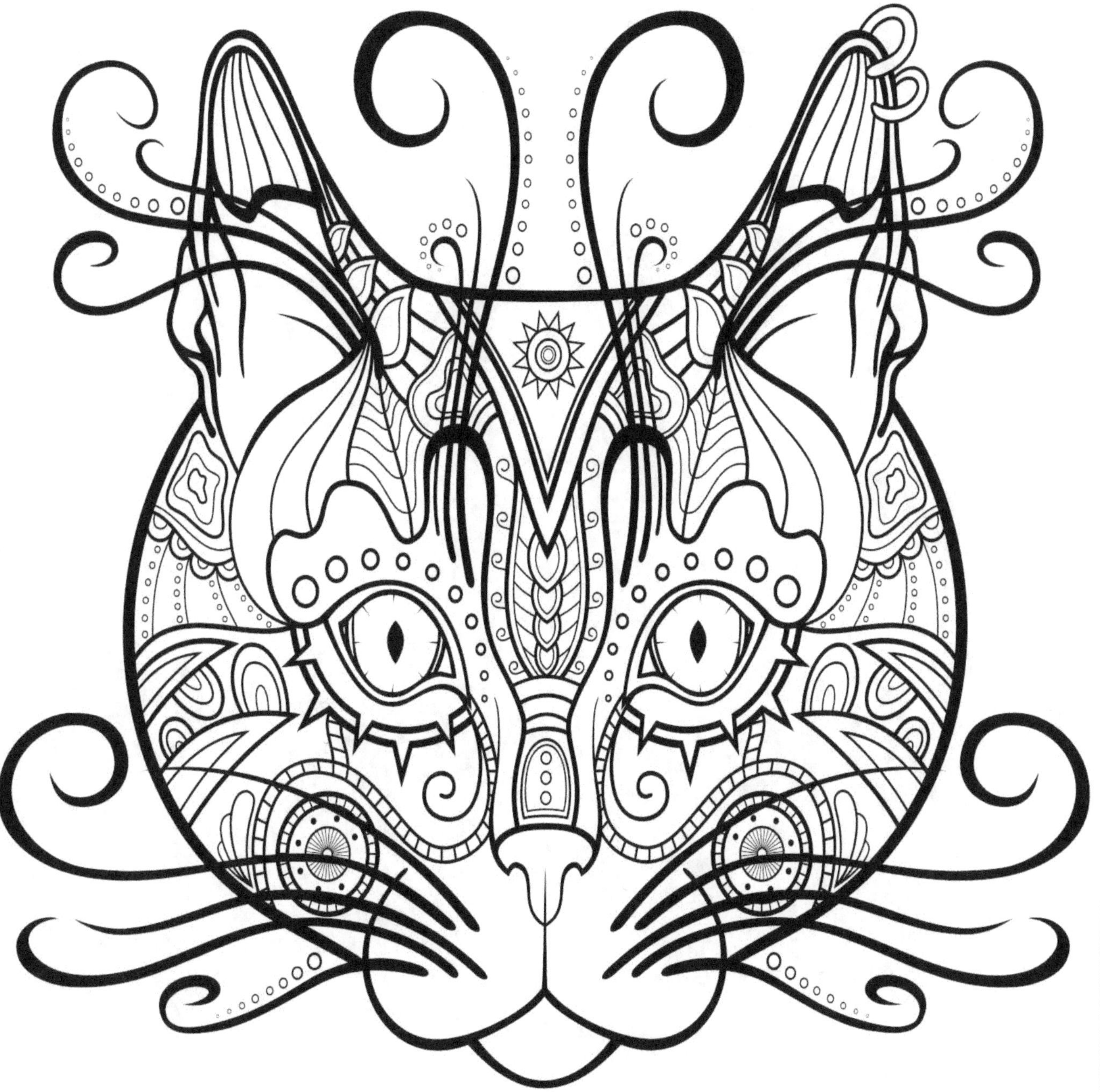

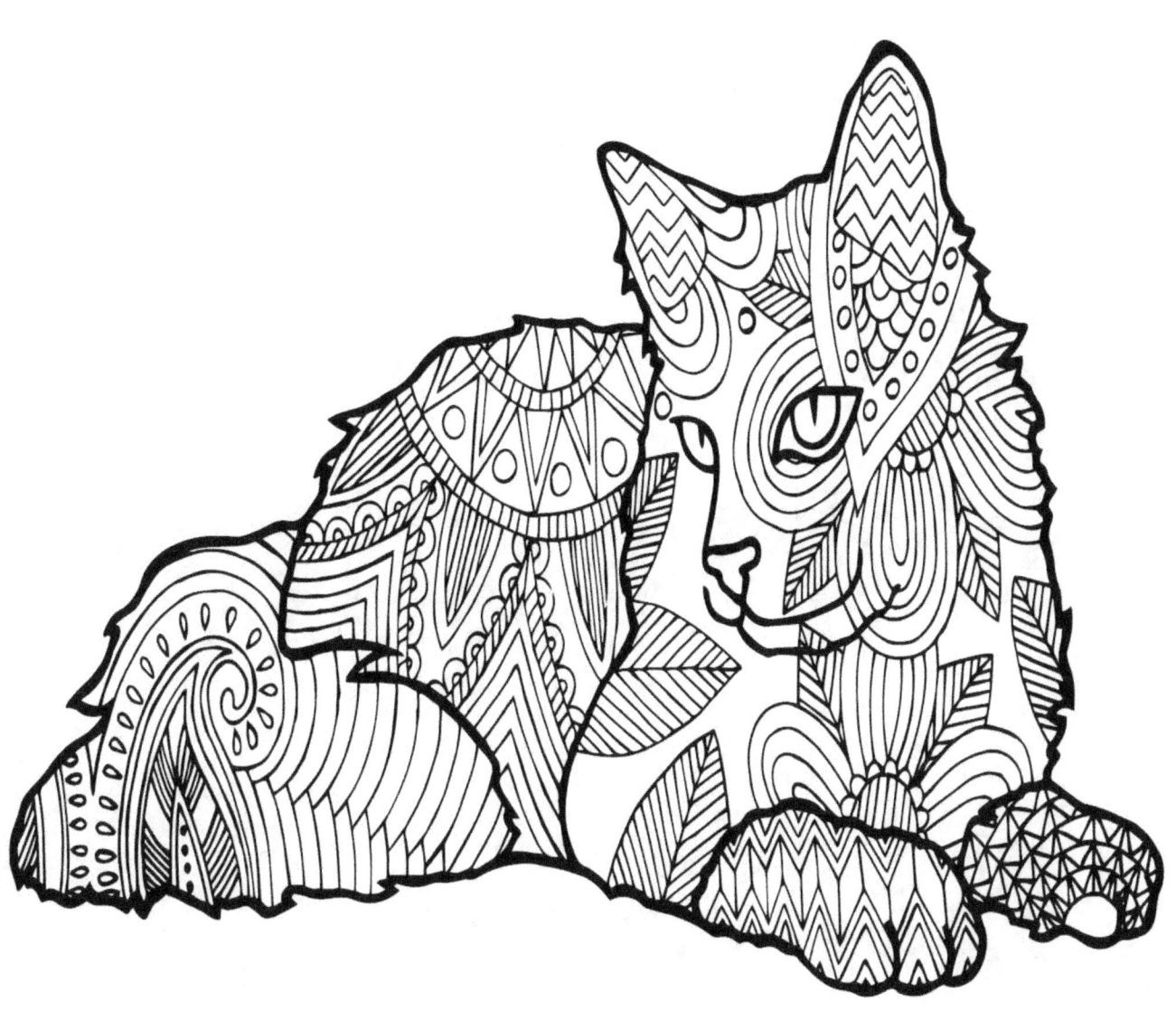

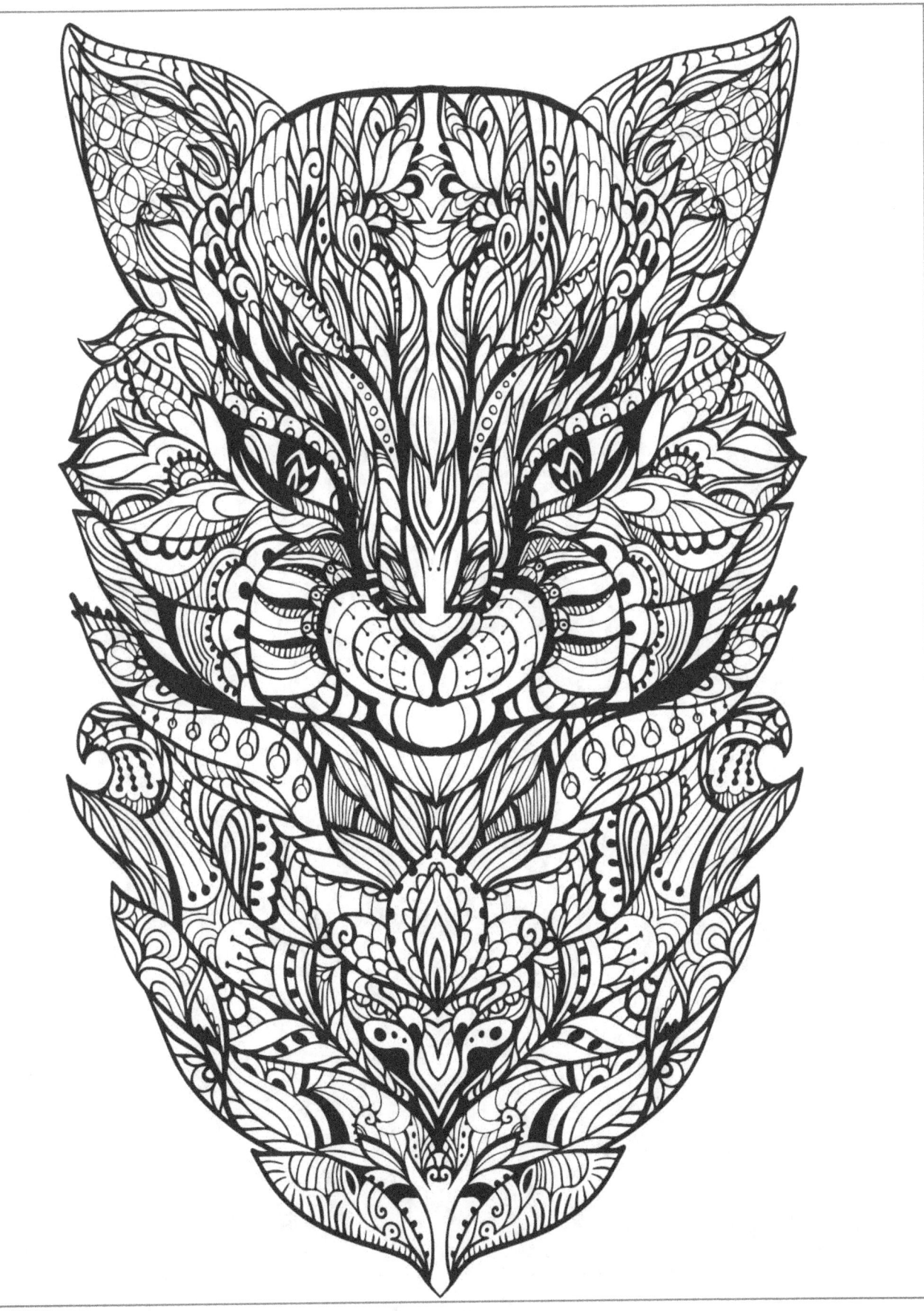

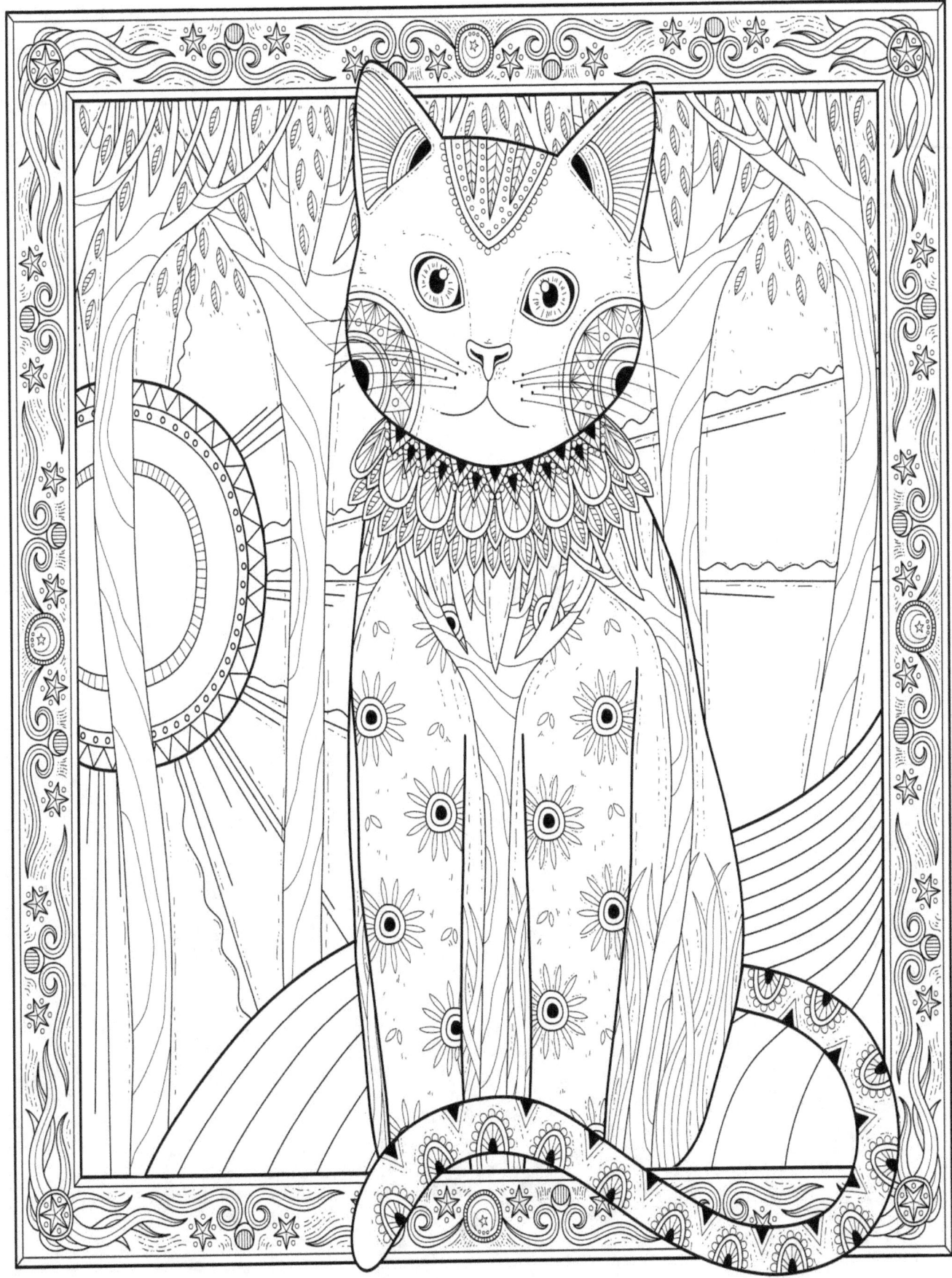

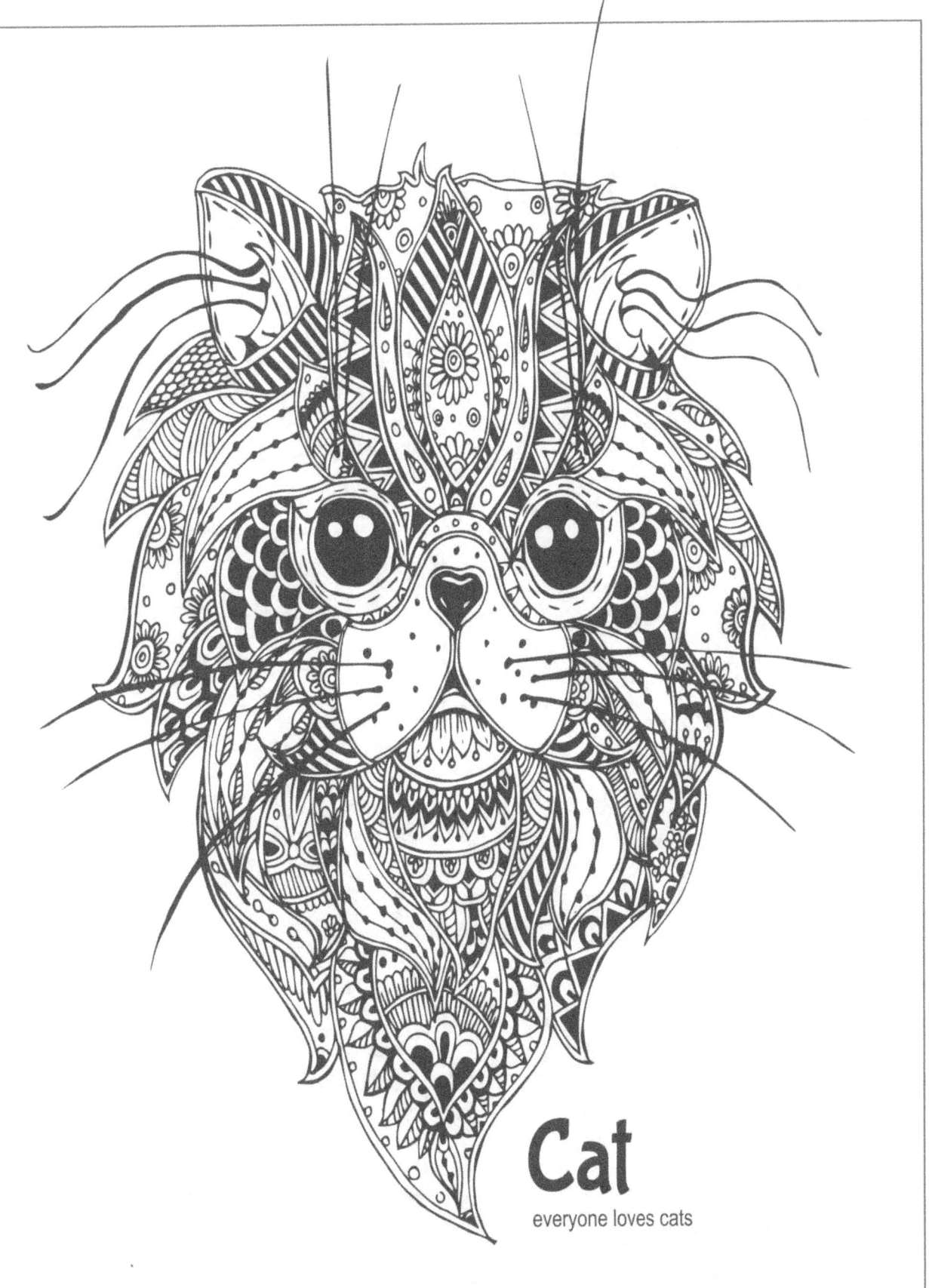

Cat

everyone loves cats

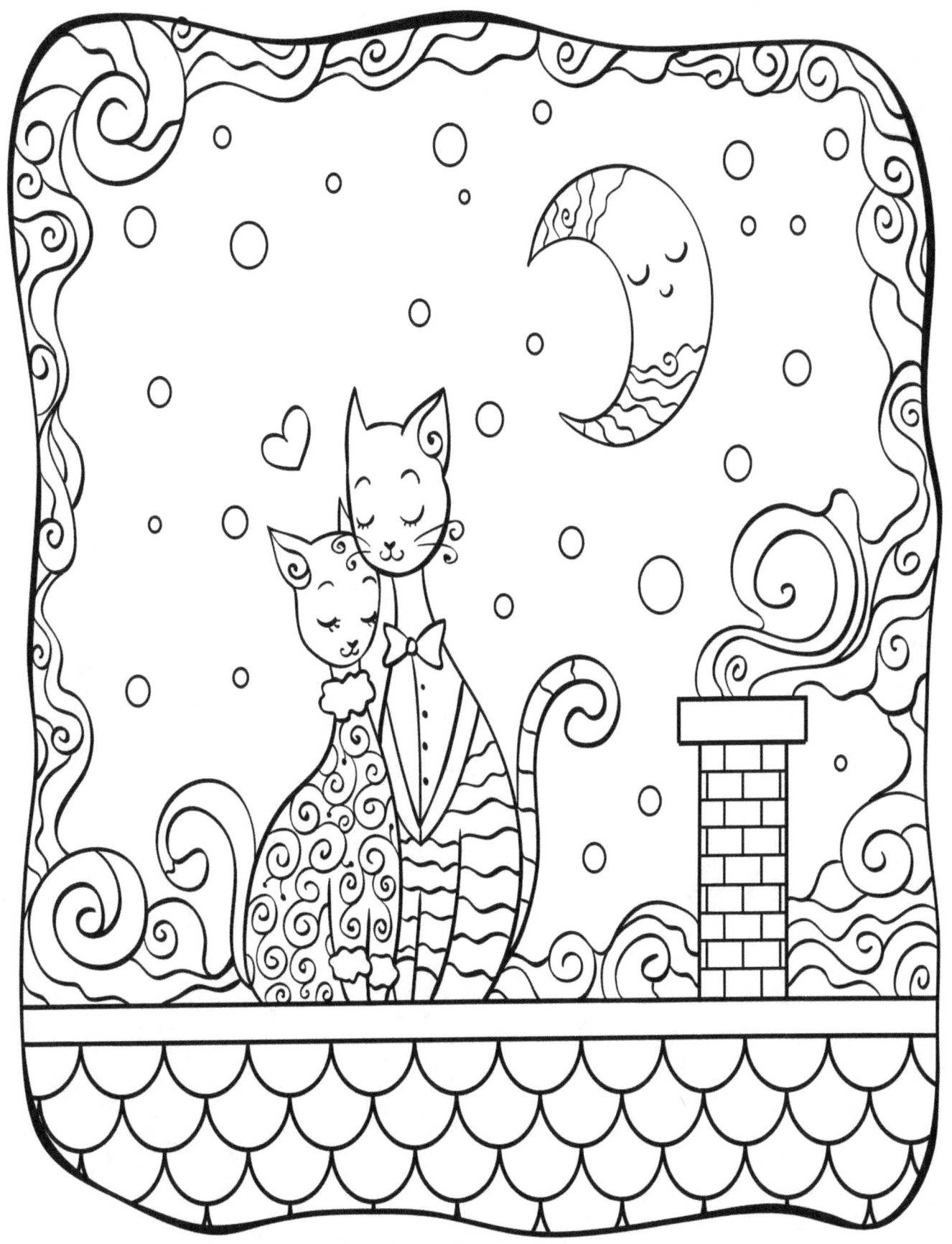

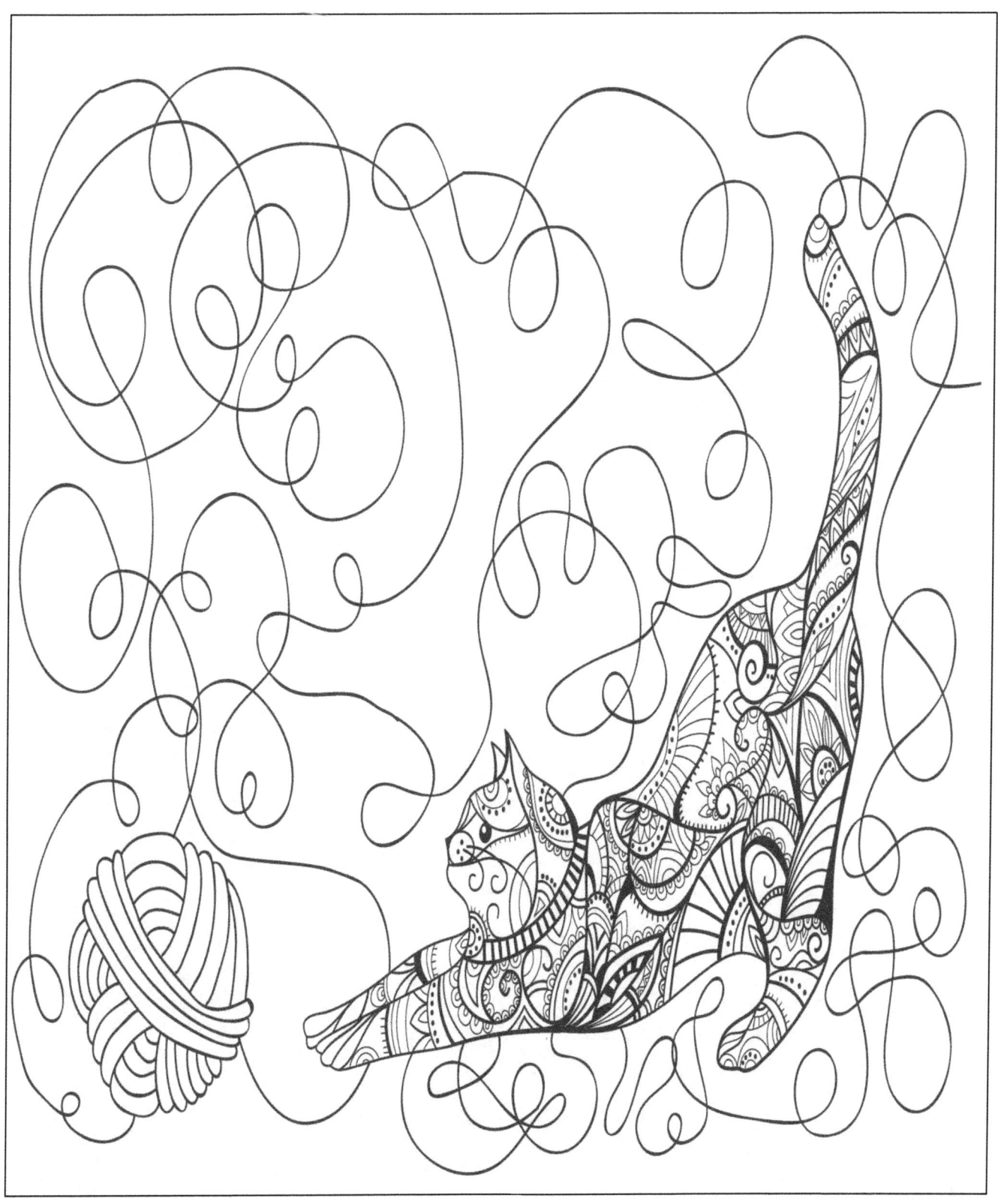

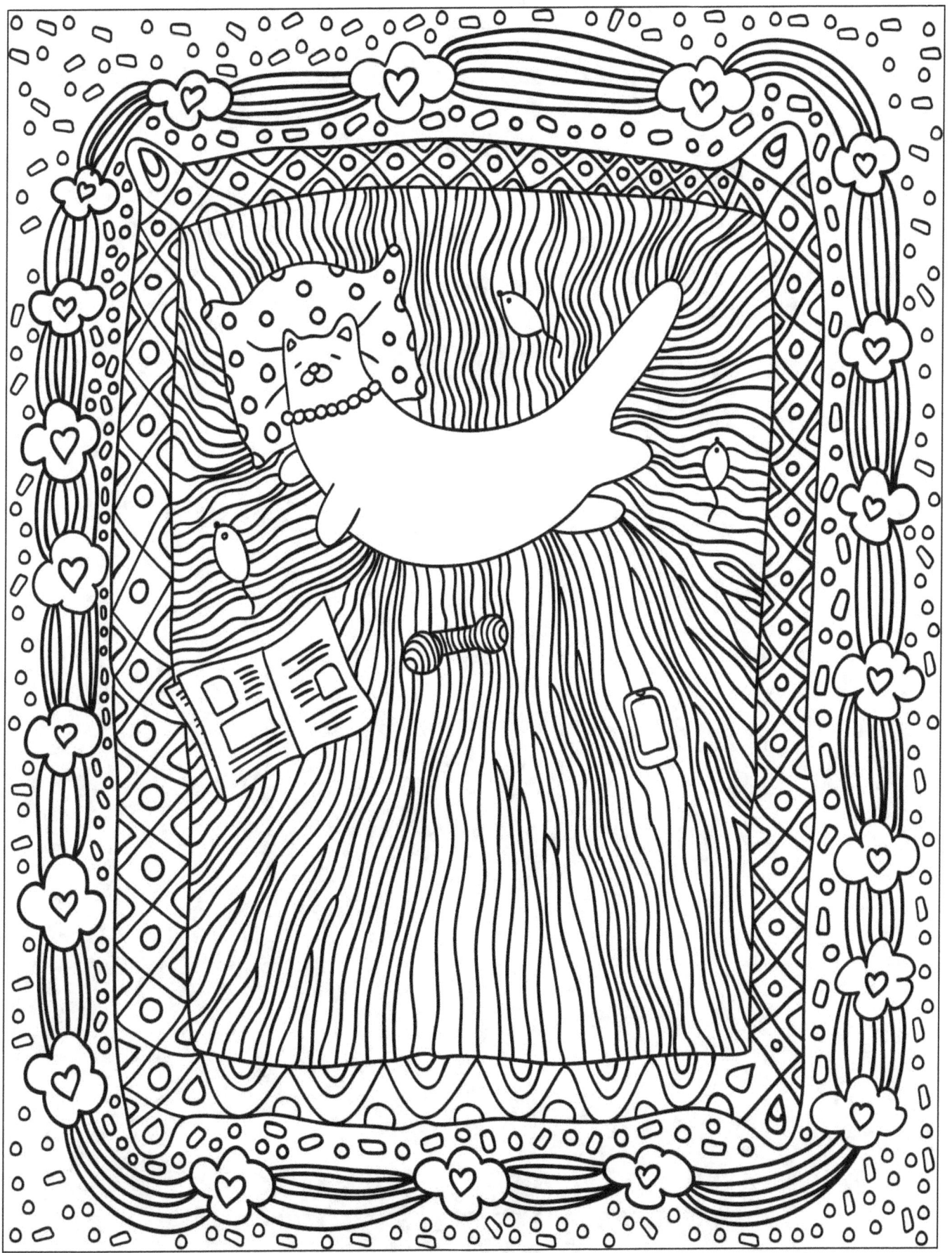

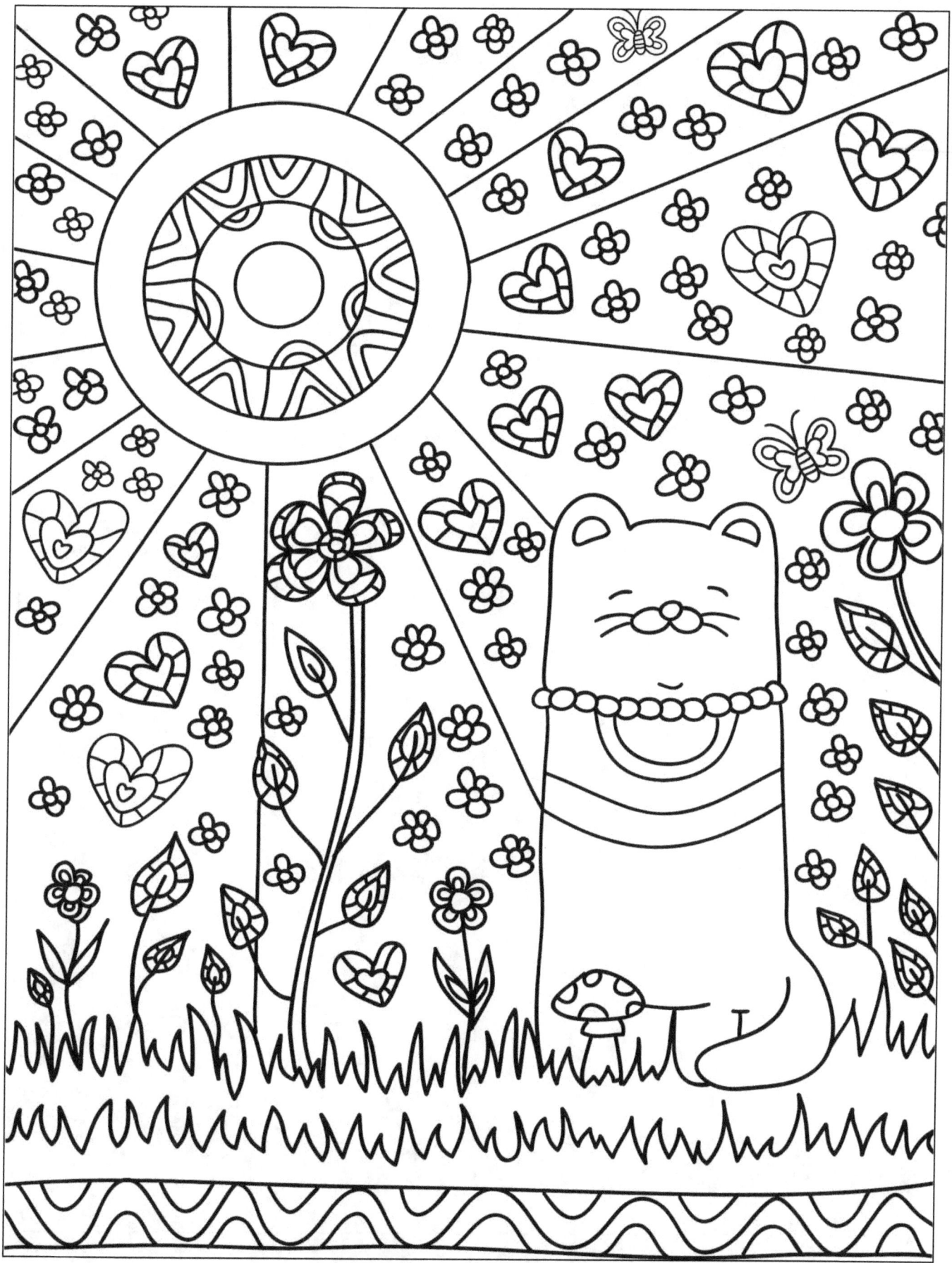

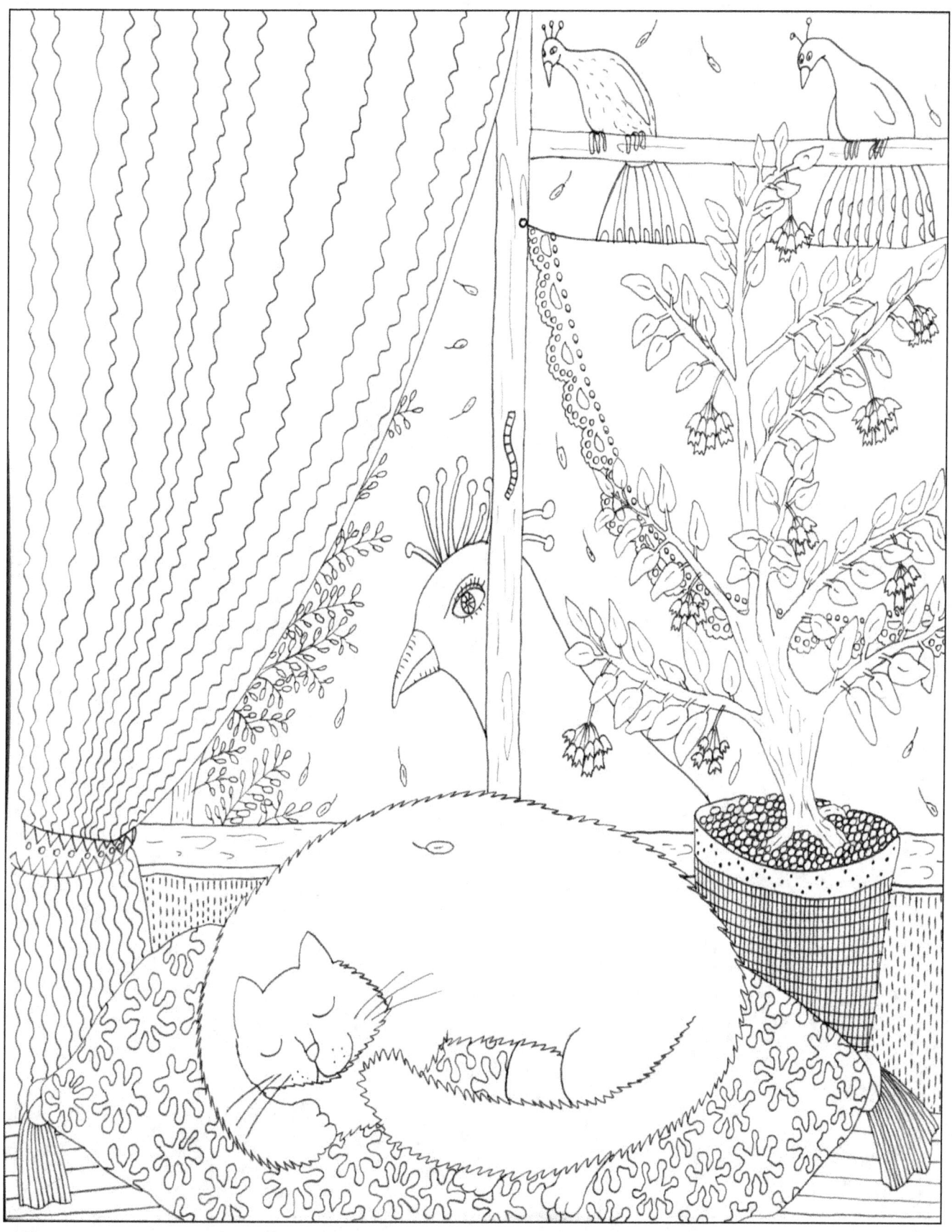

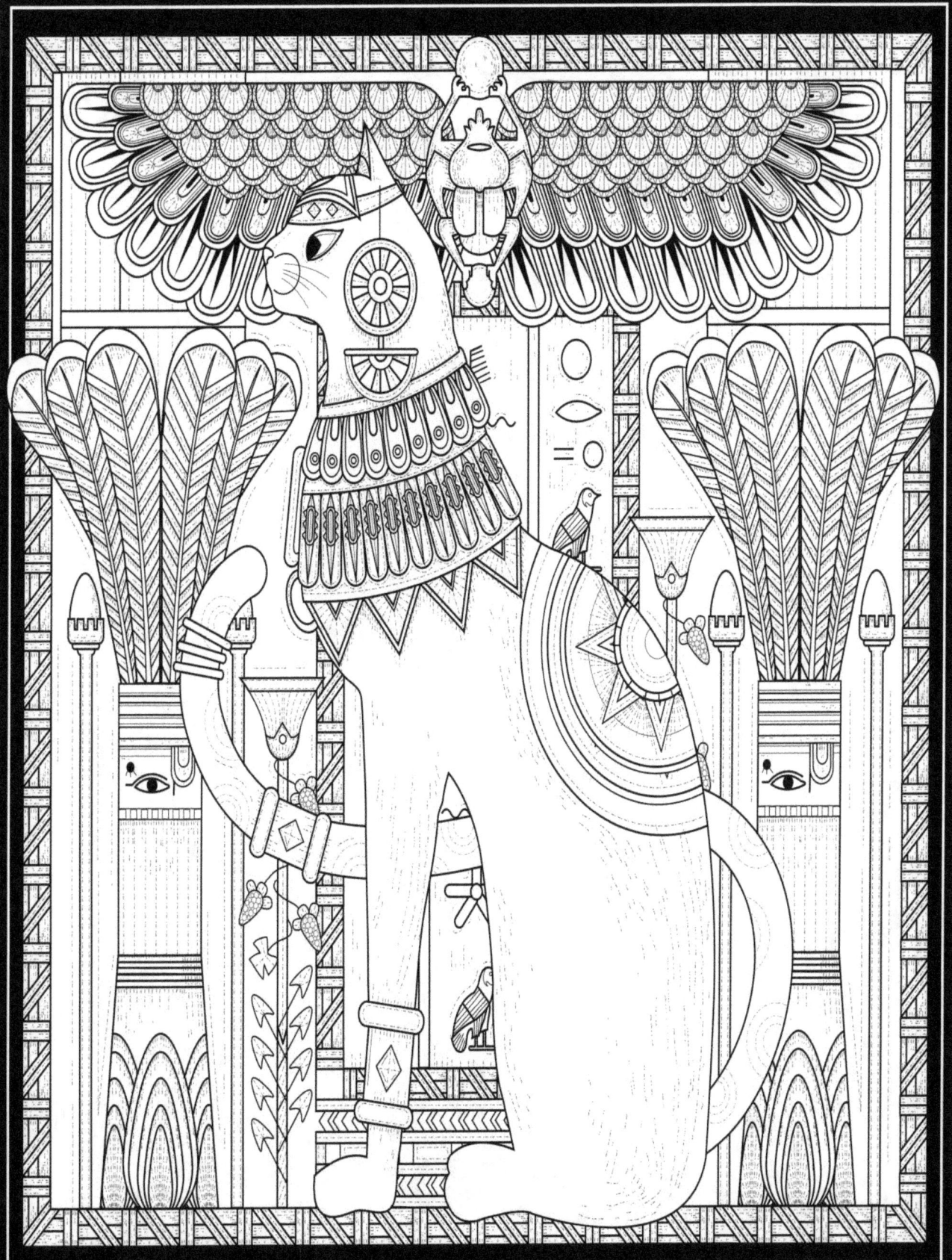

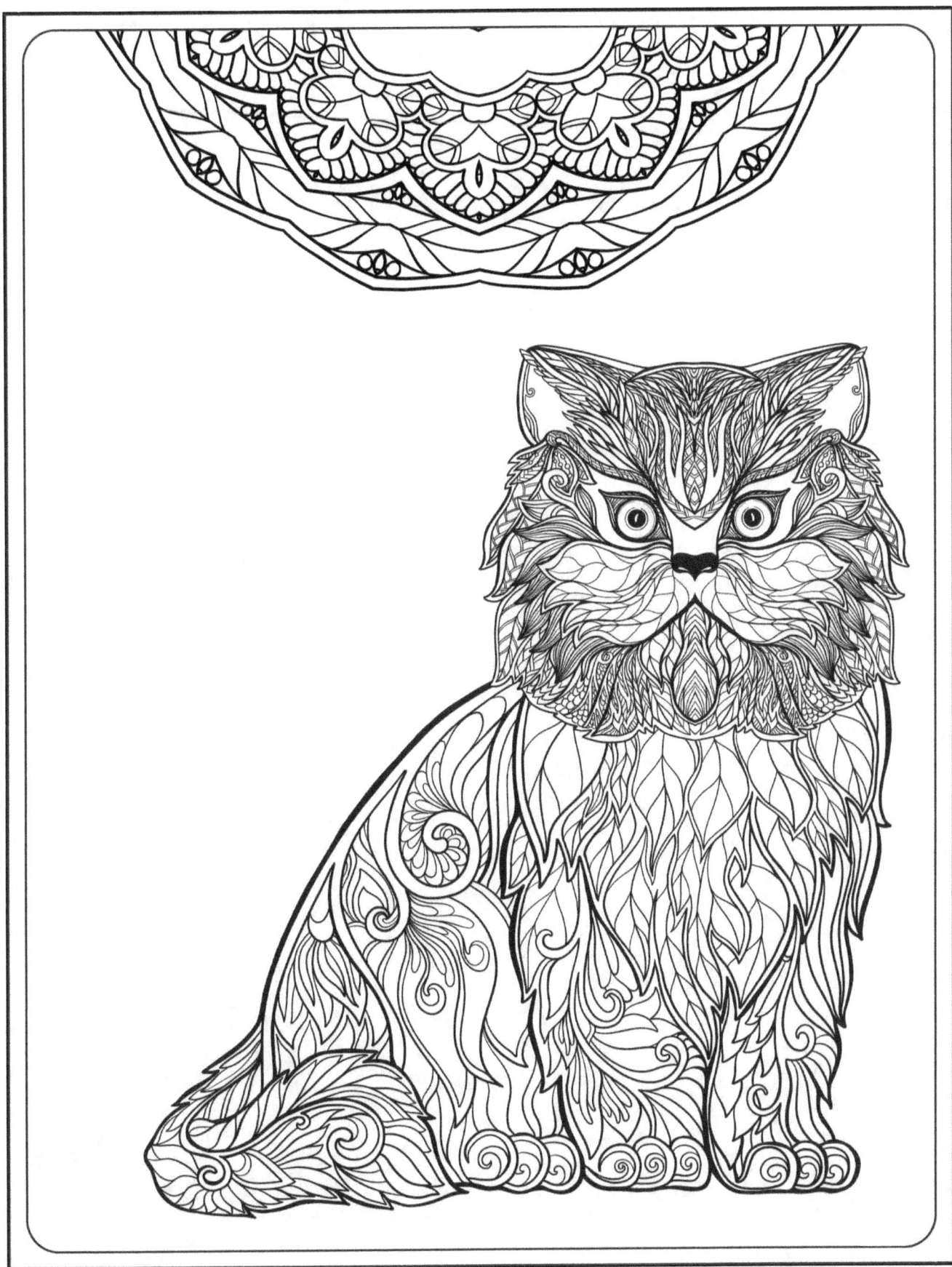

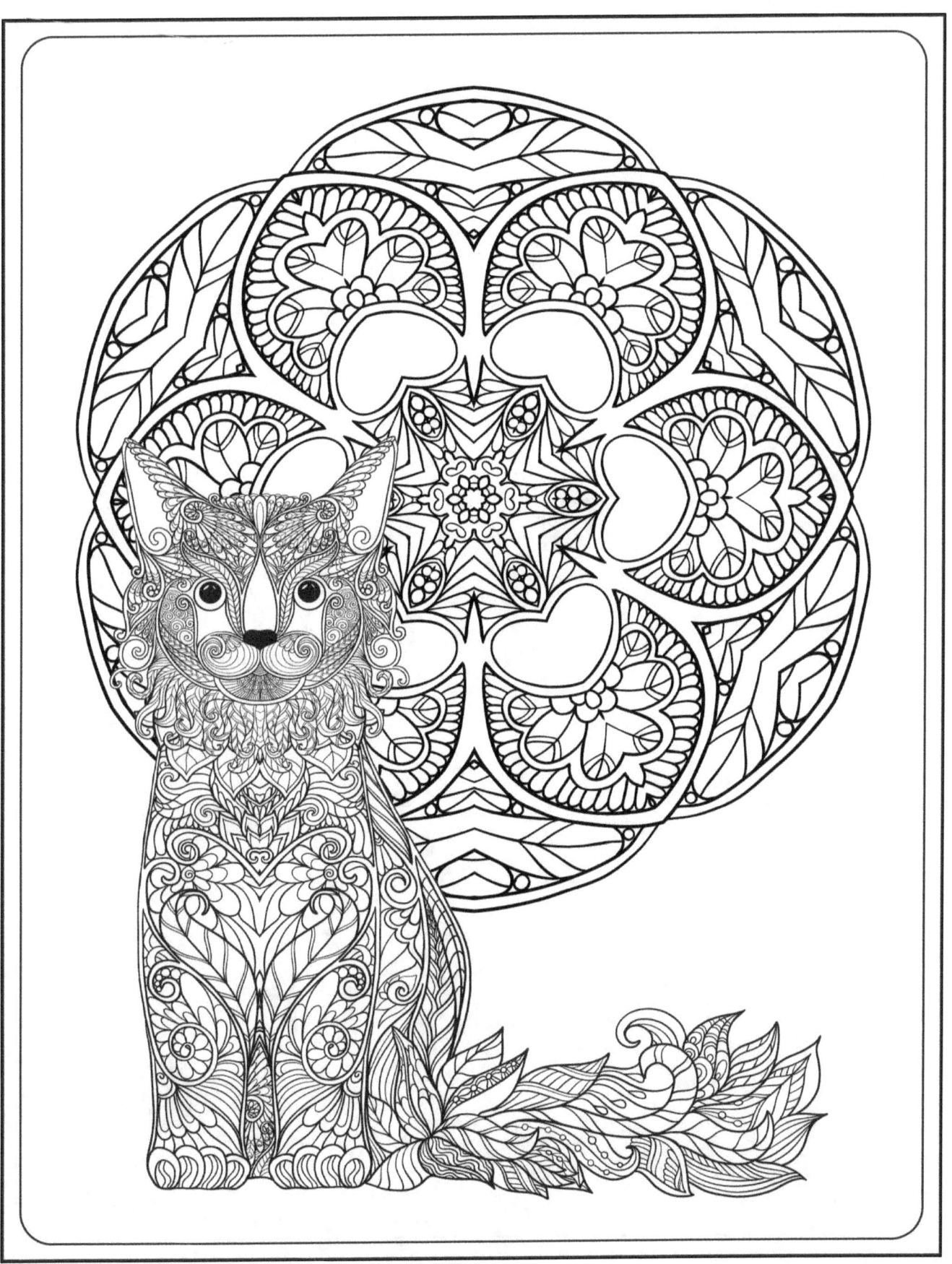

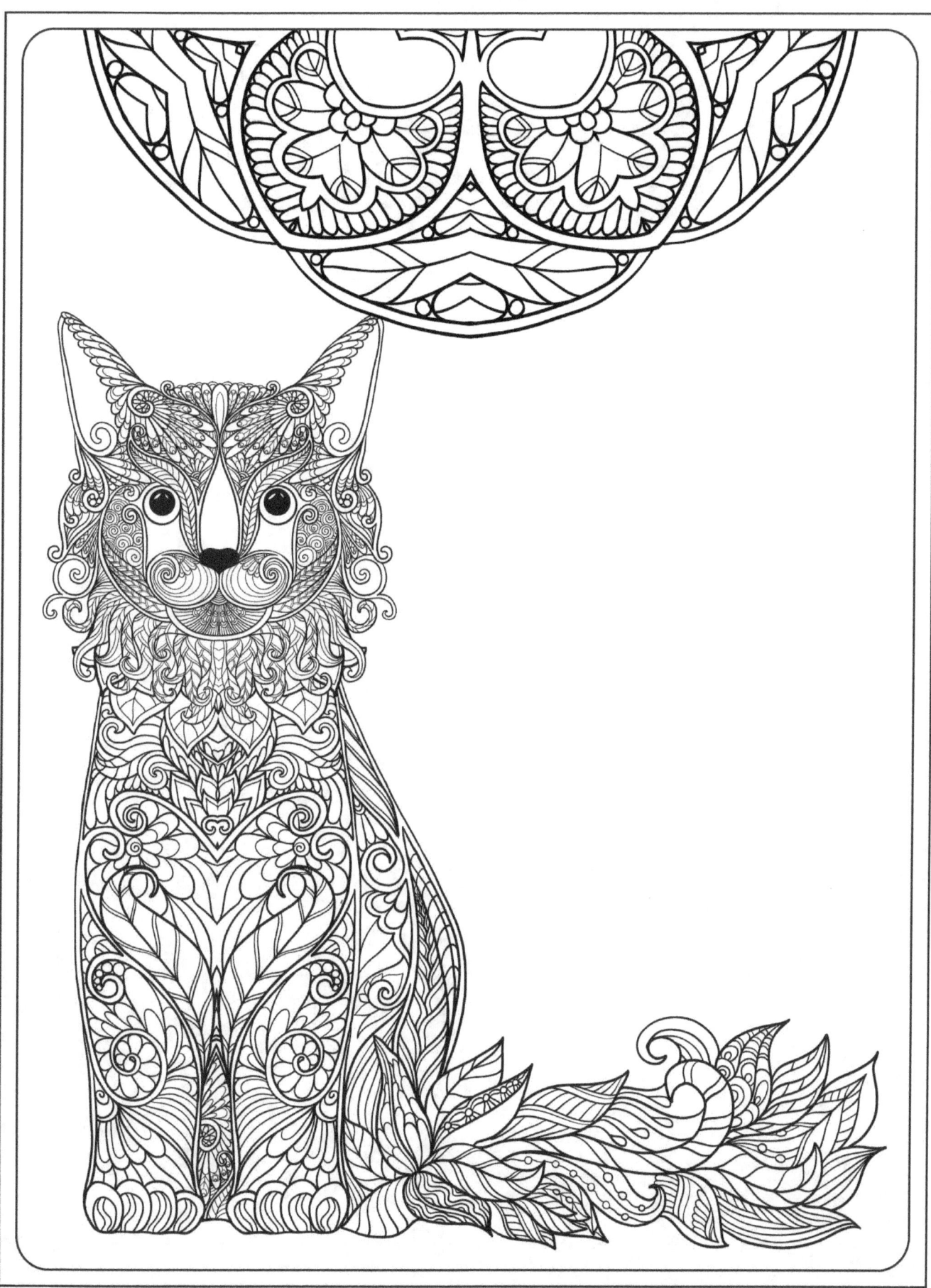

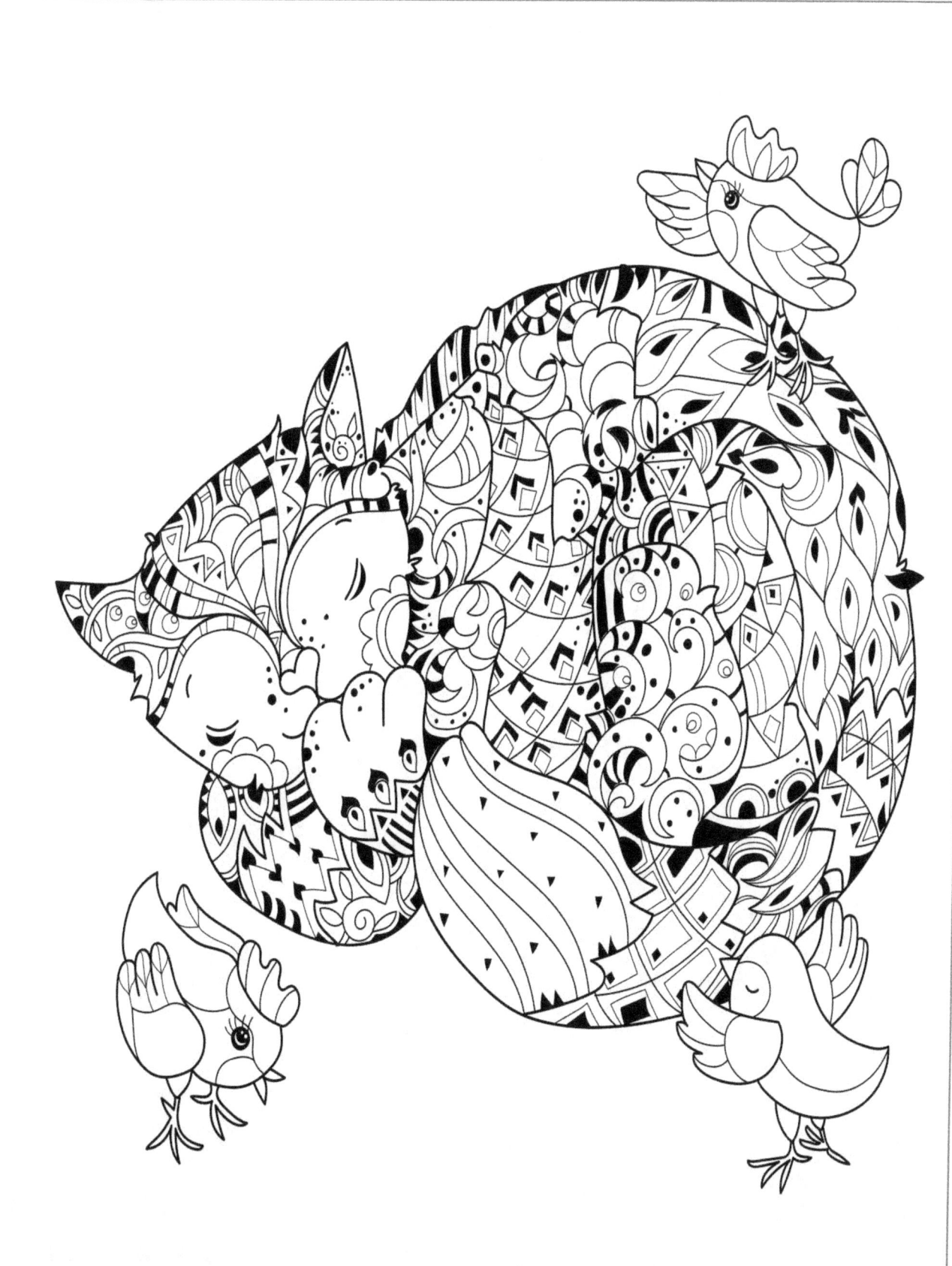

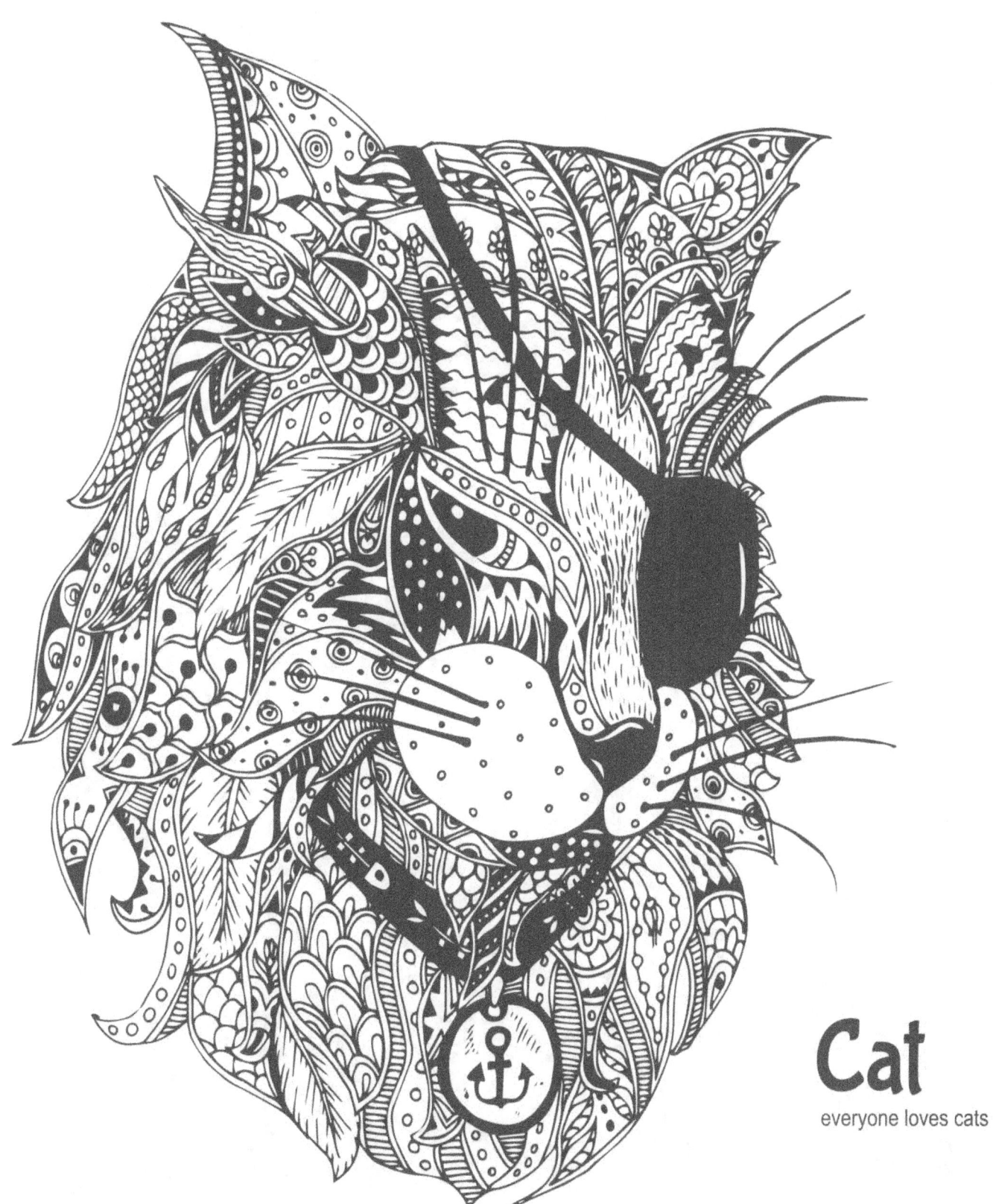

Cat
everyone loves cats

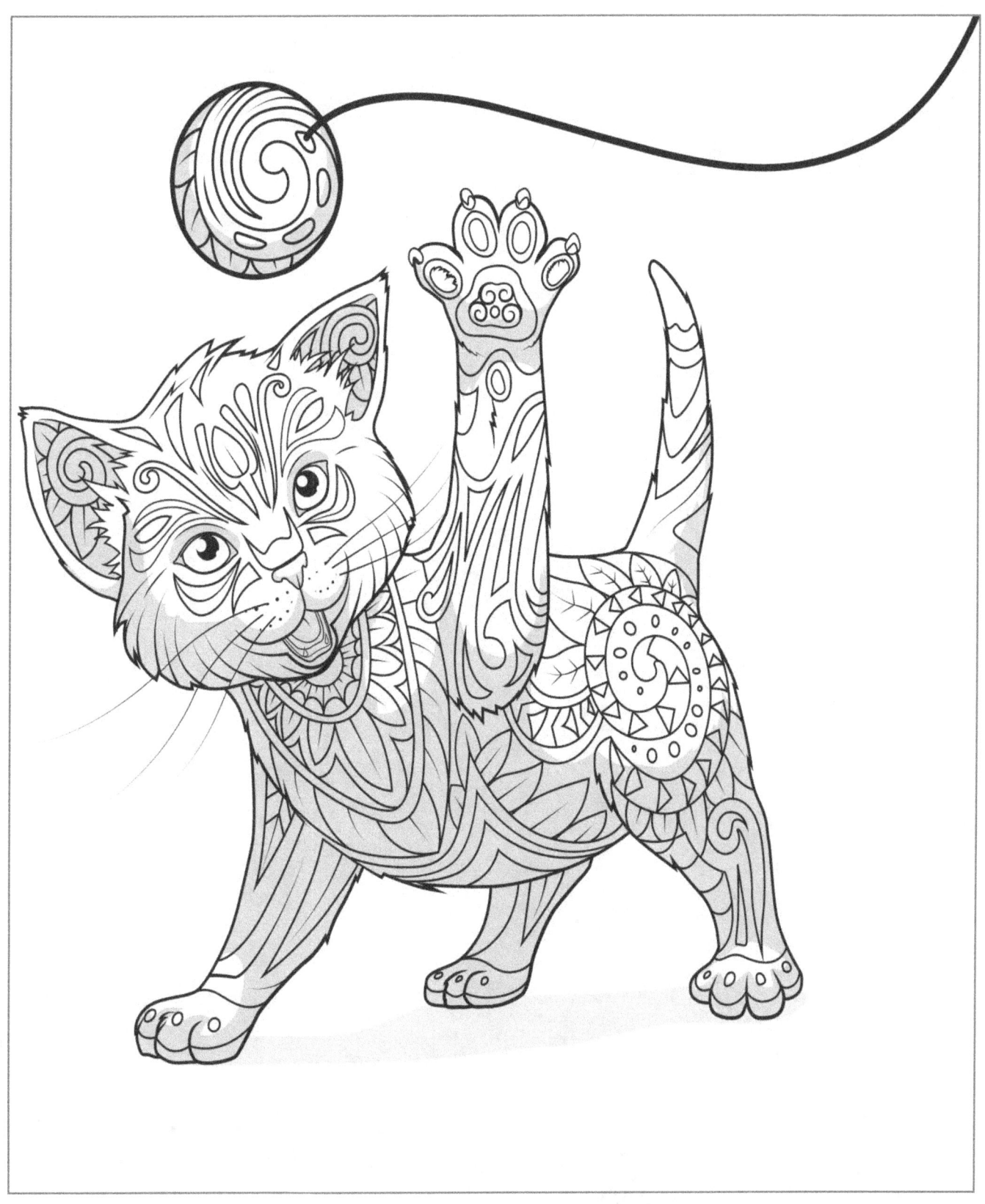

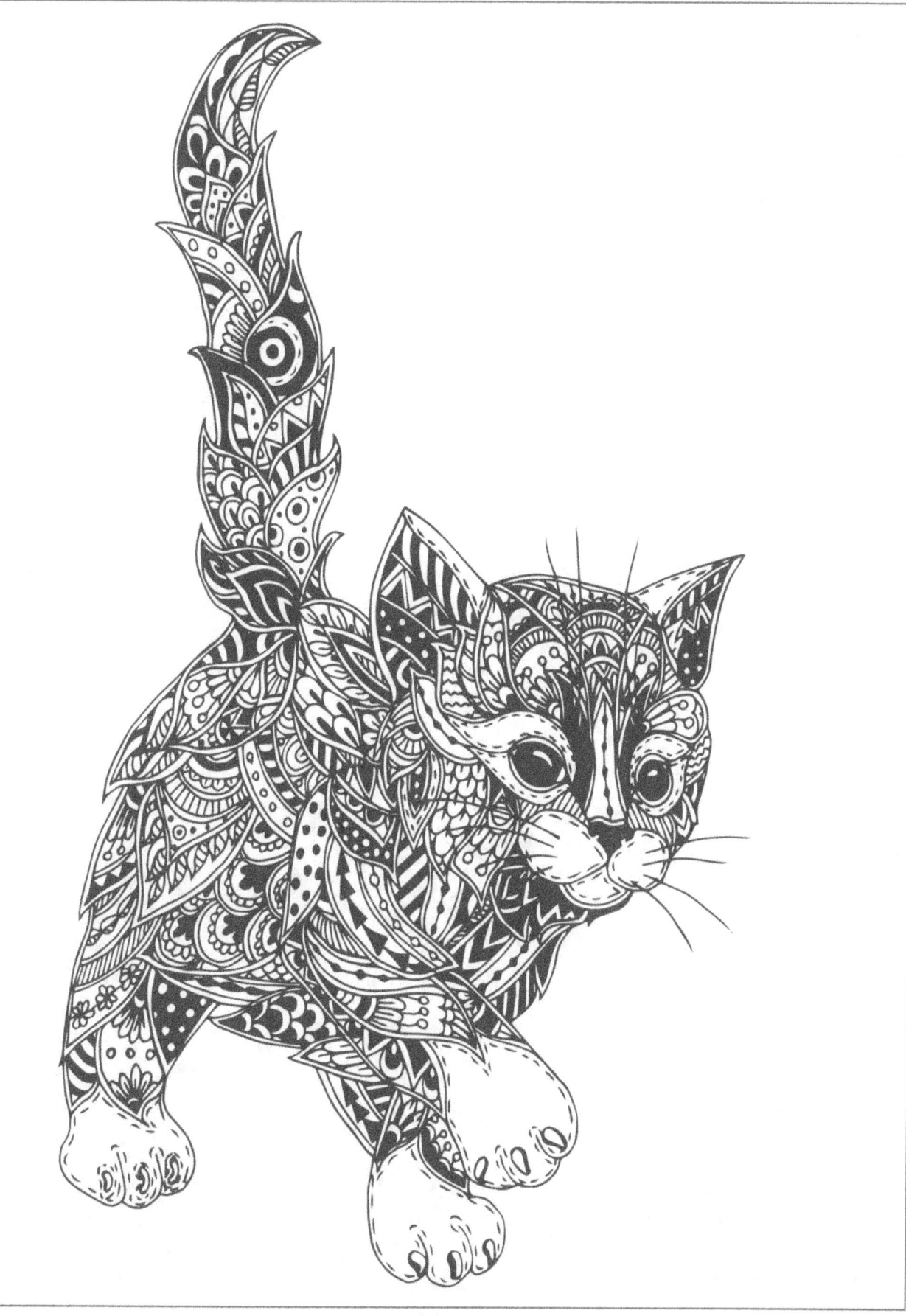

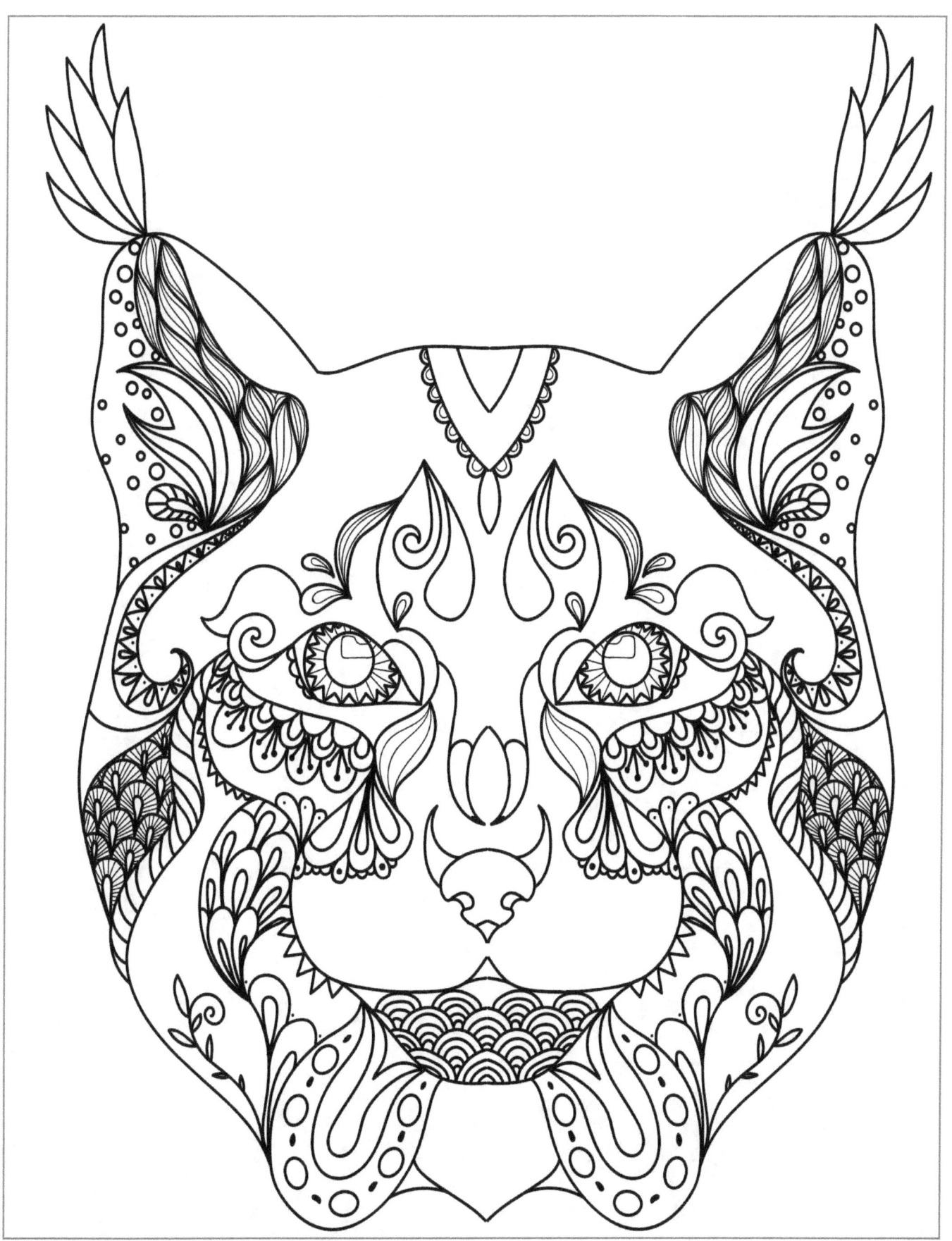

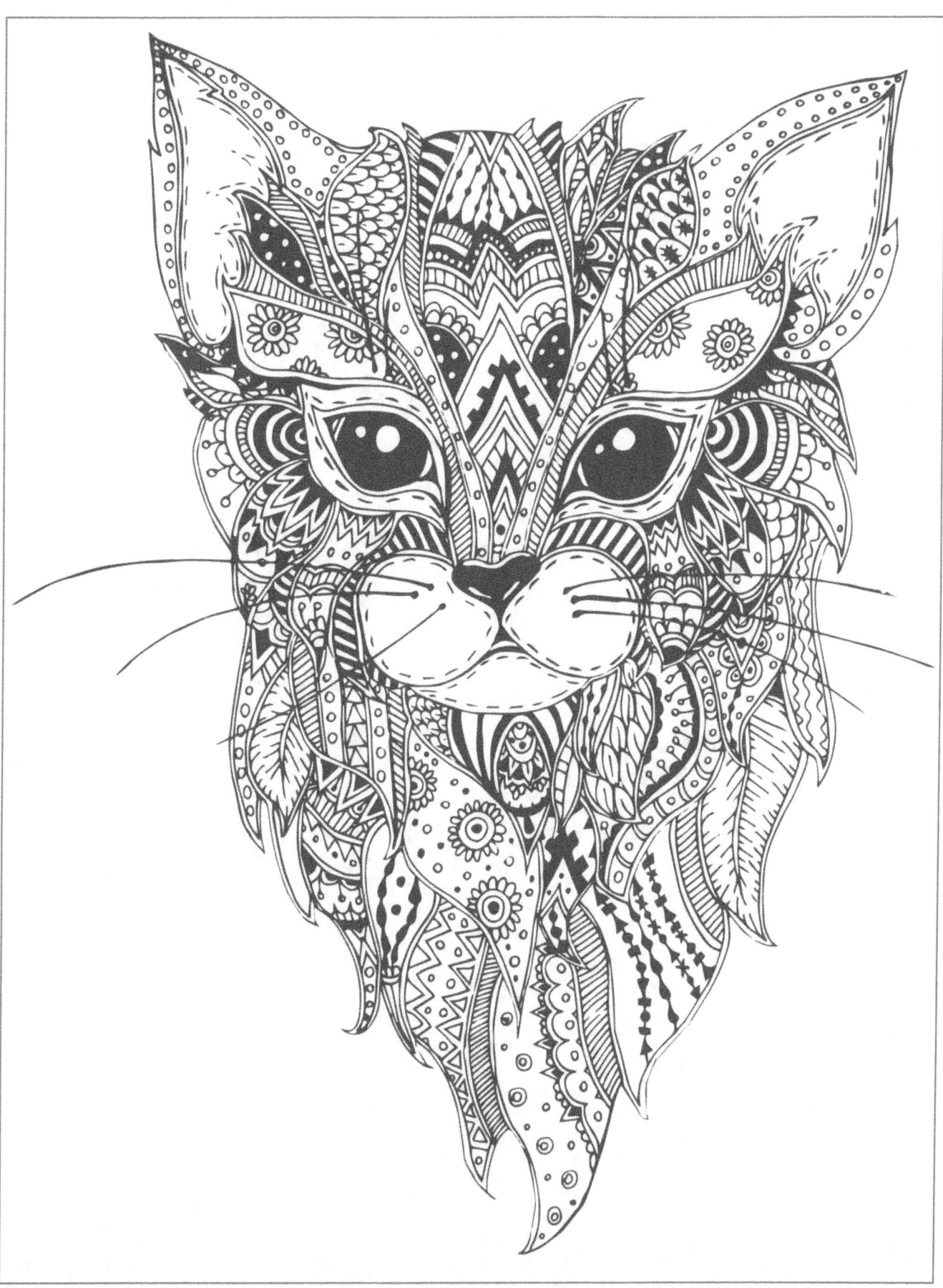

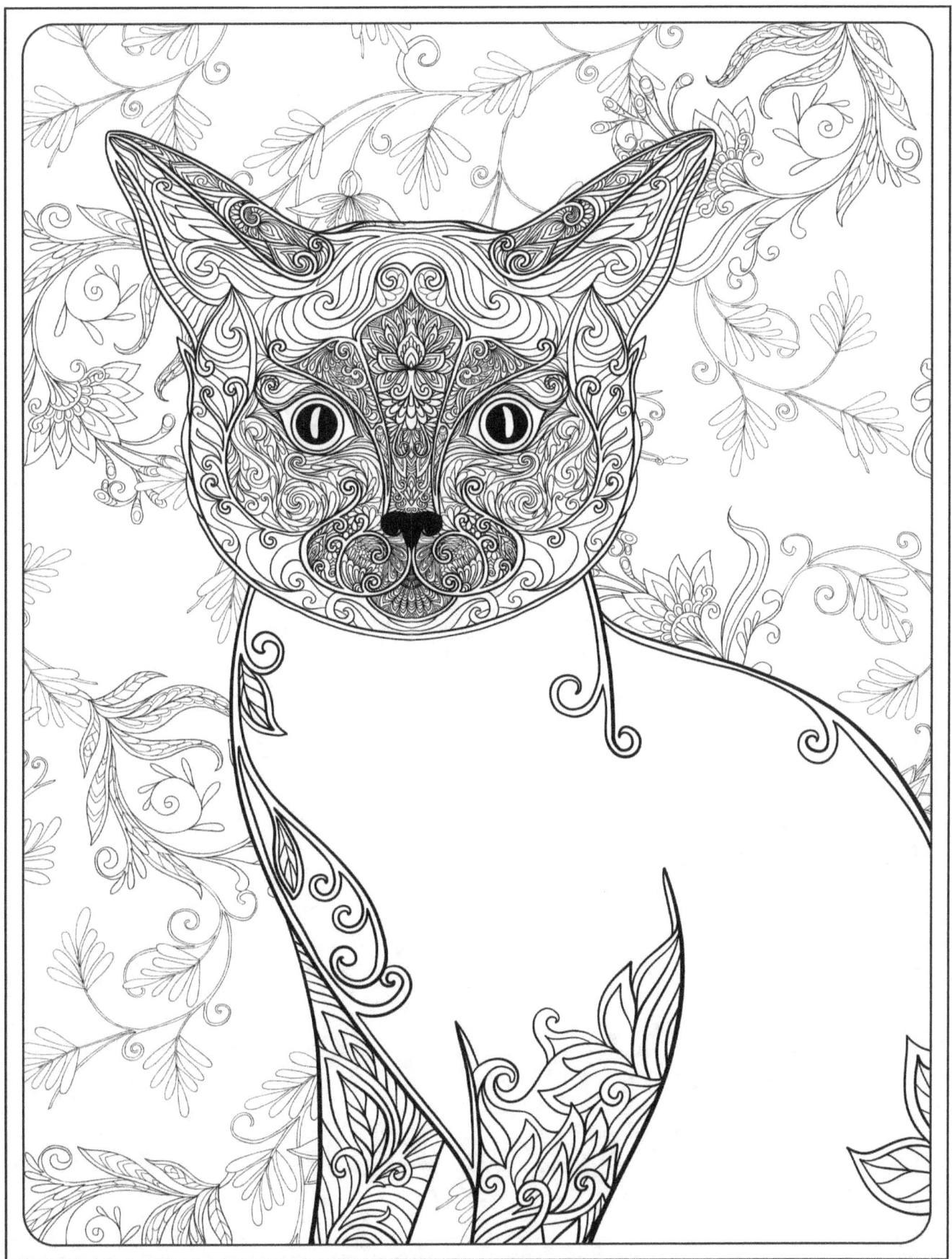

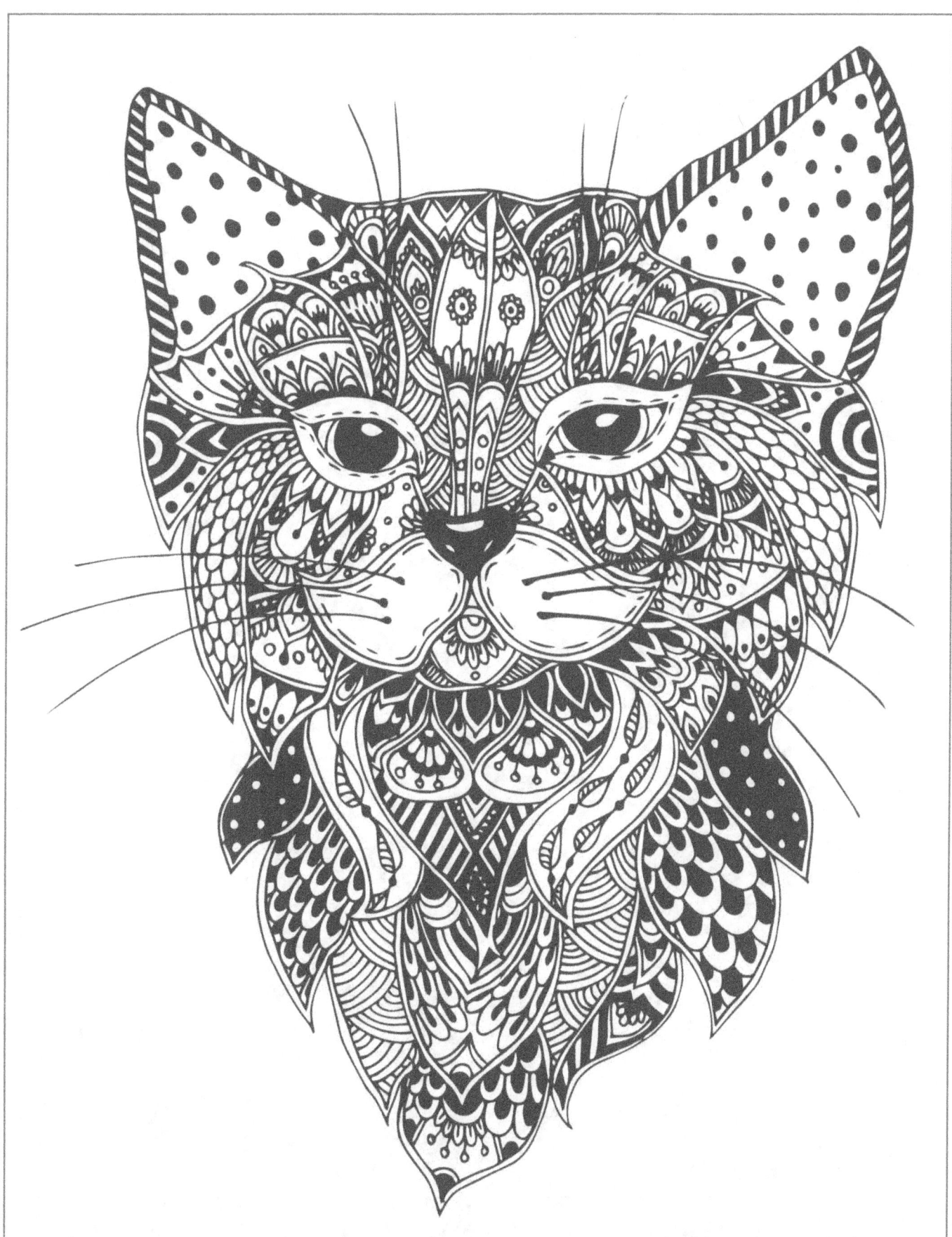

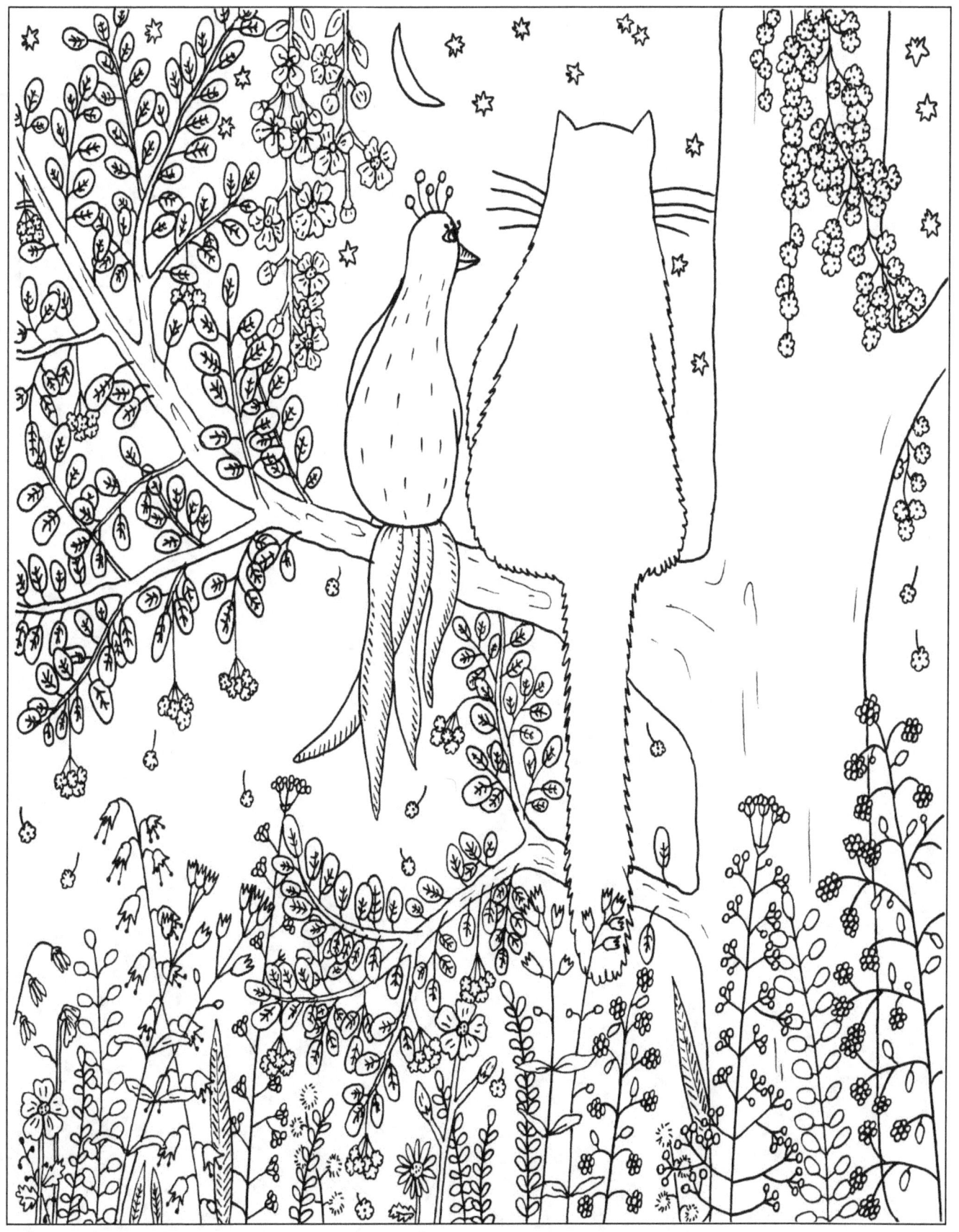

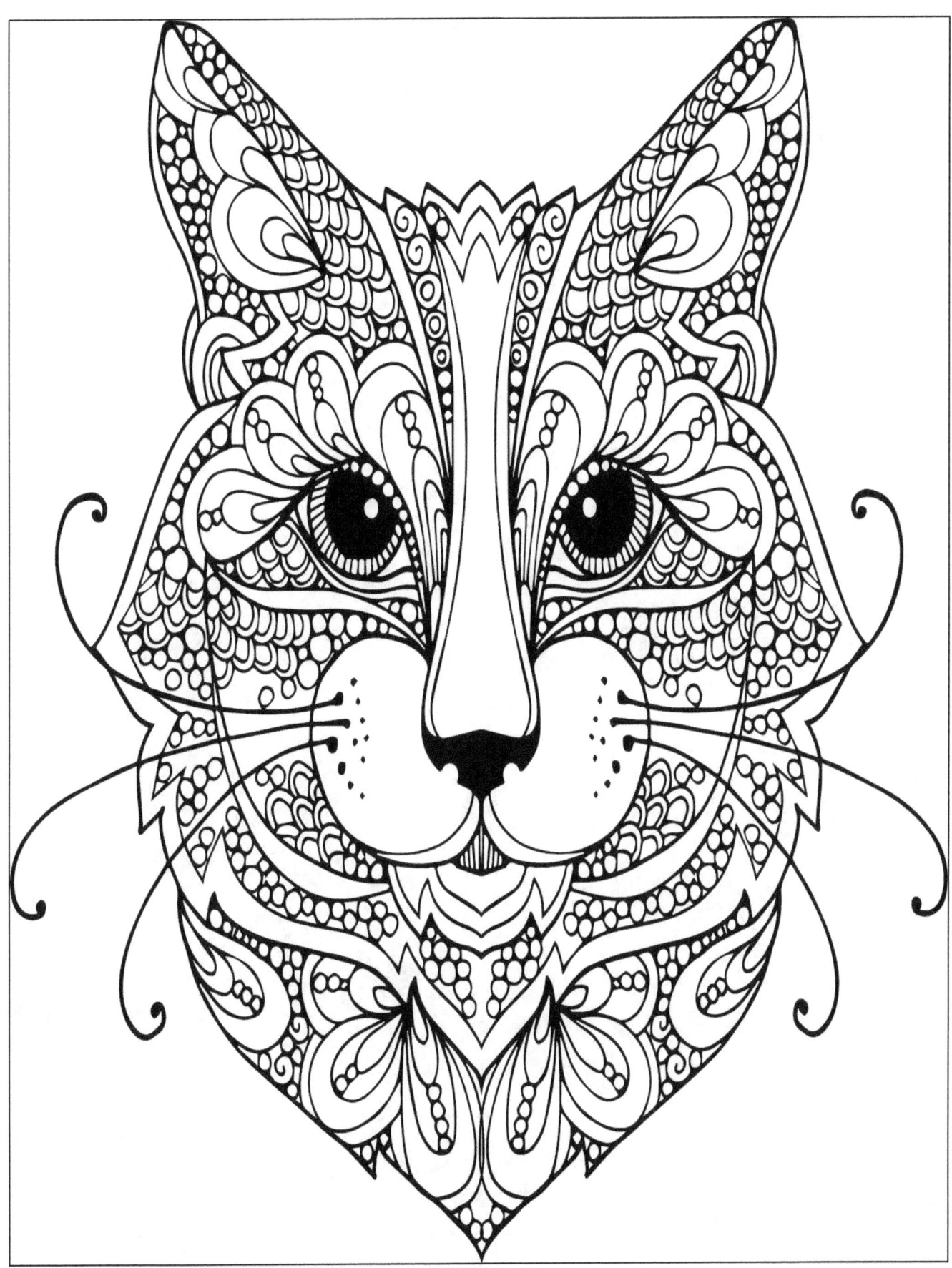

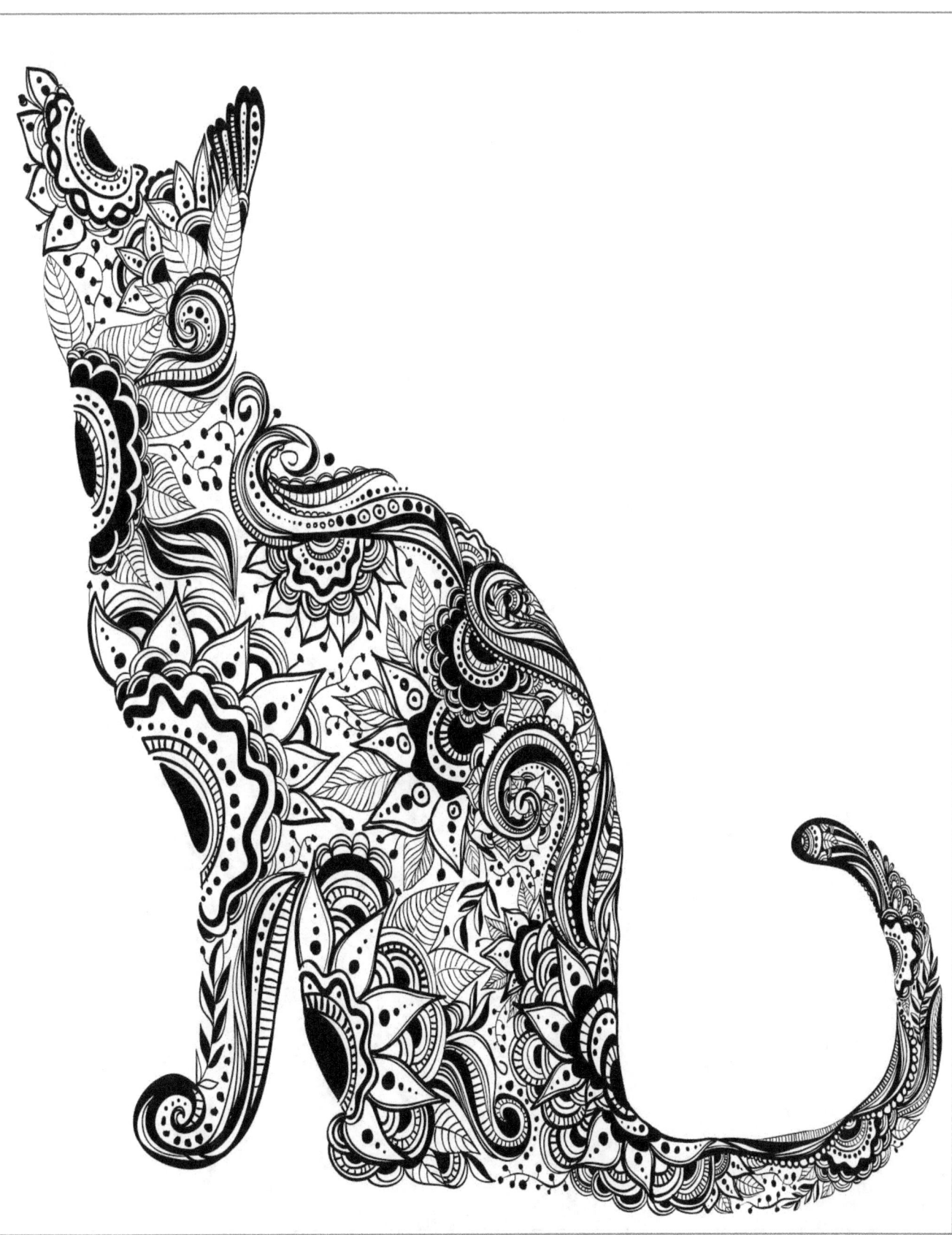

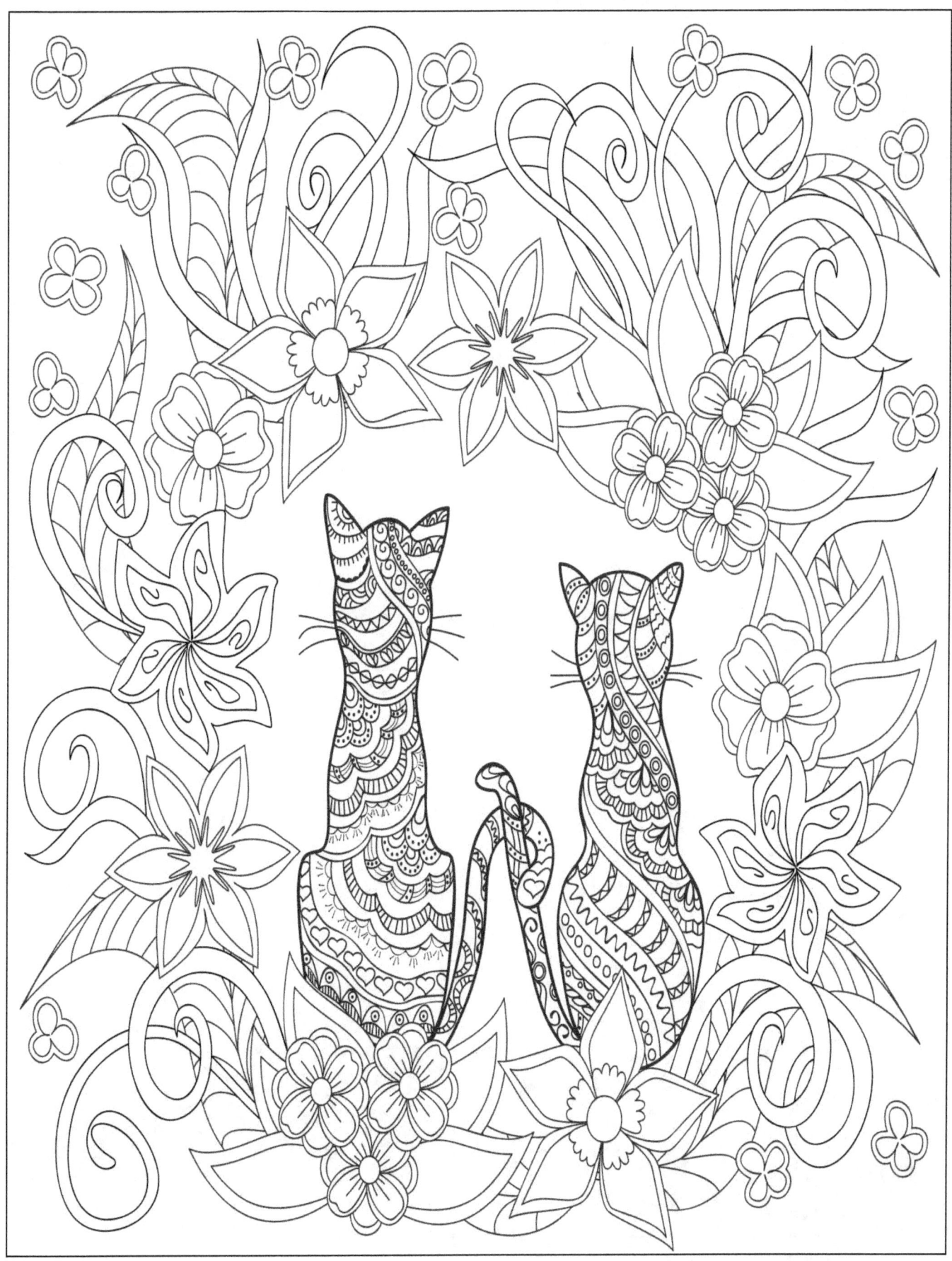

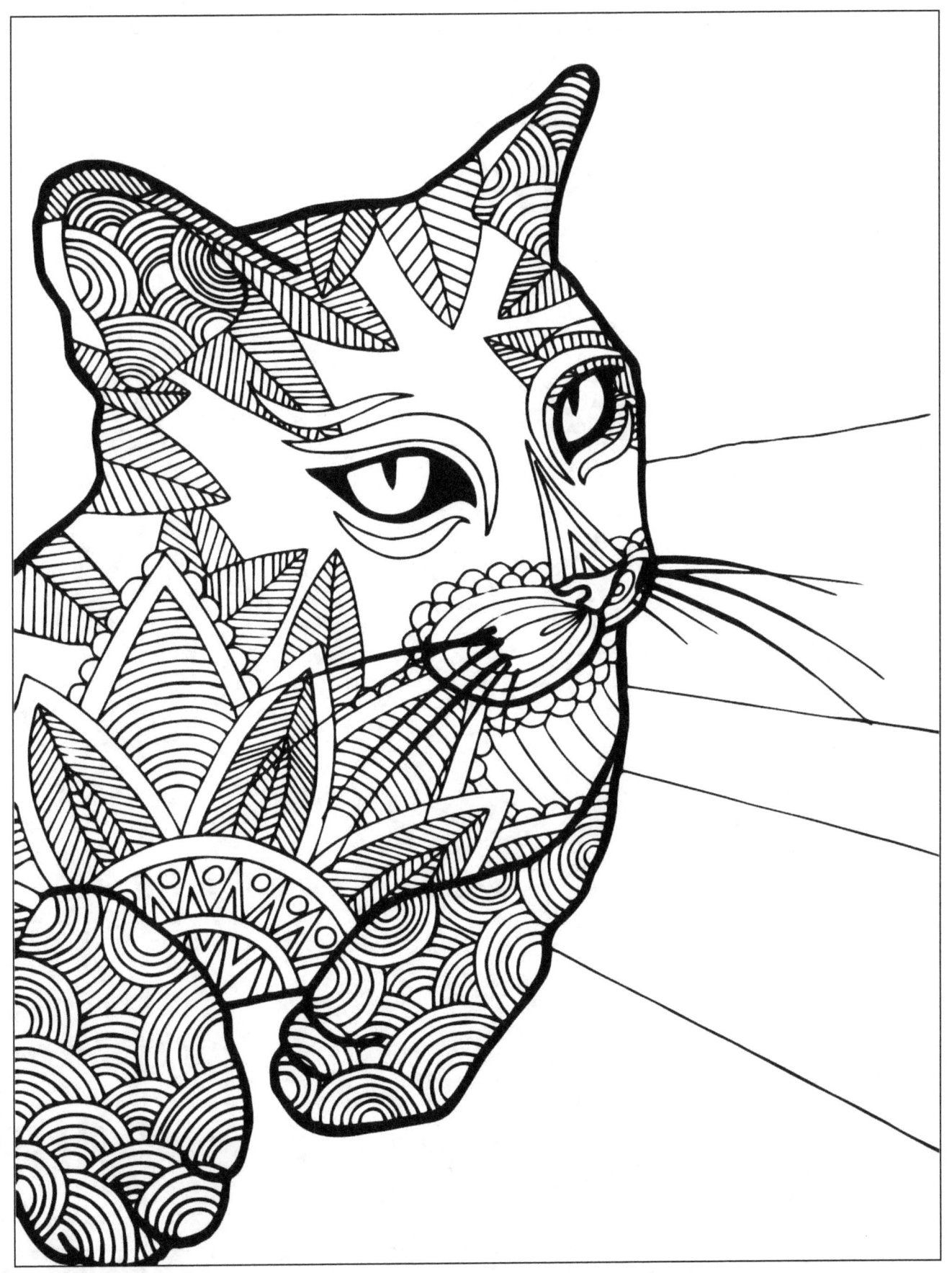

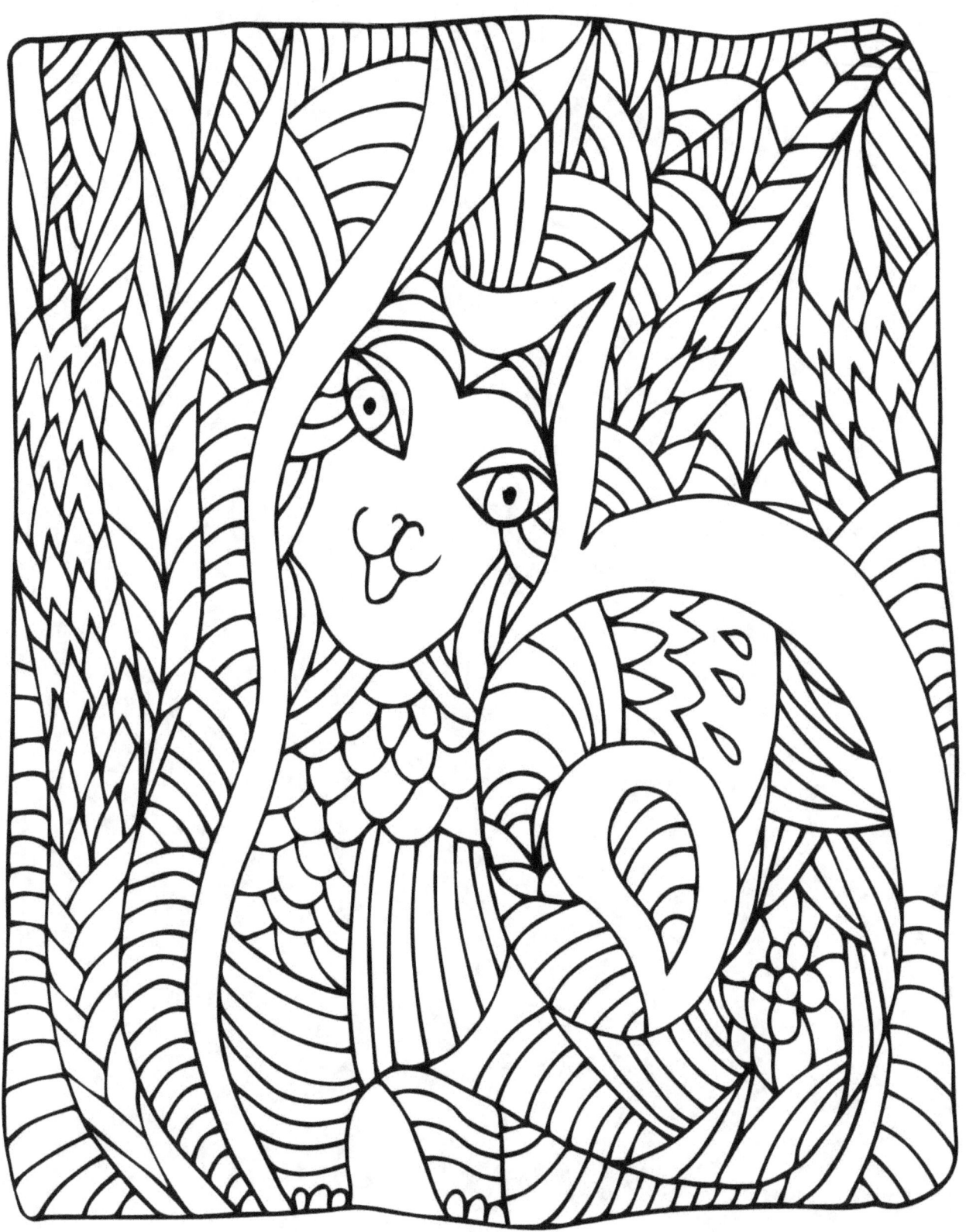

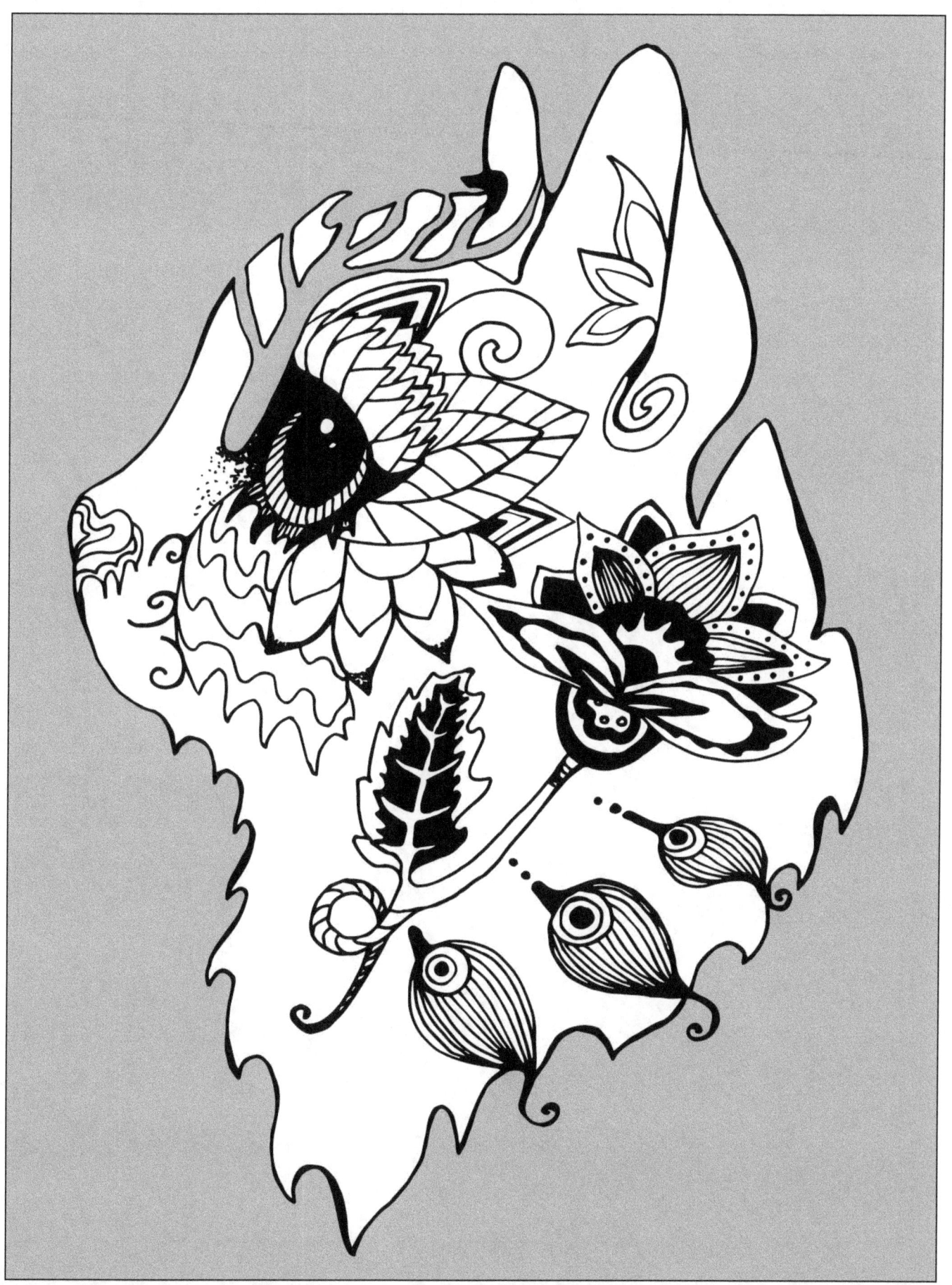

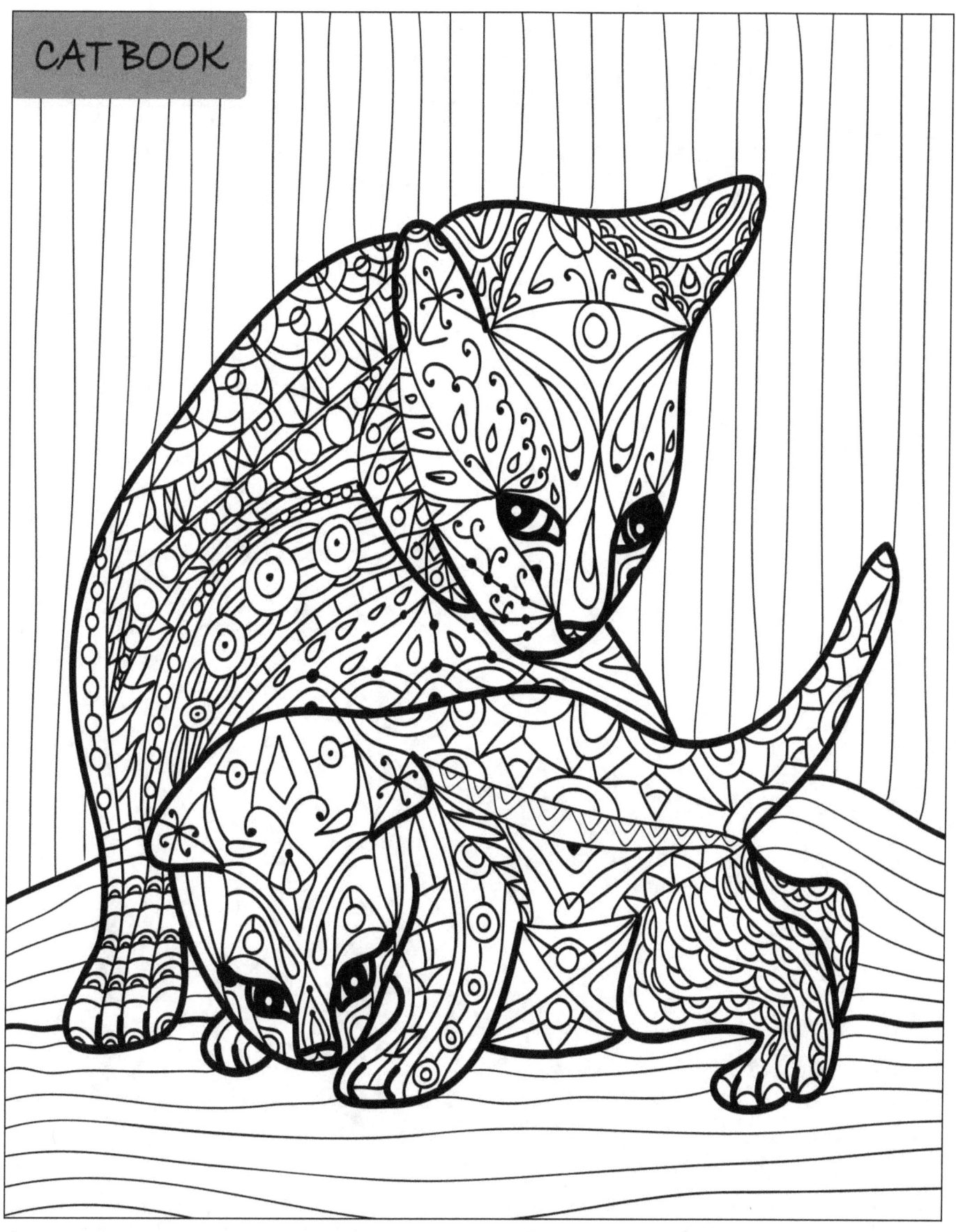

CAT BOOK

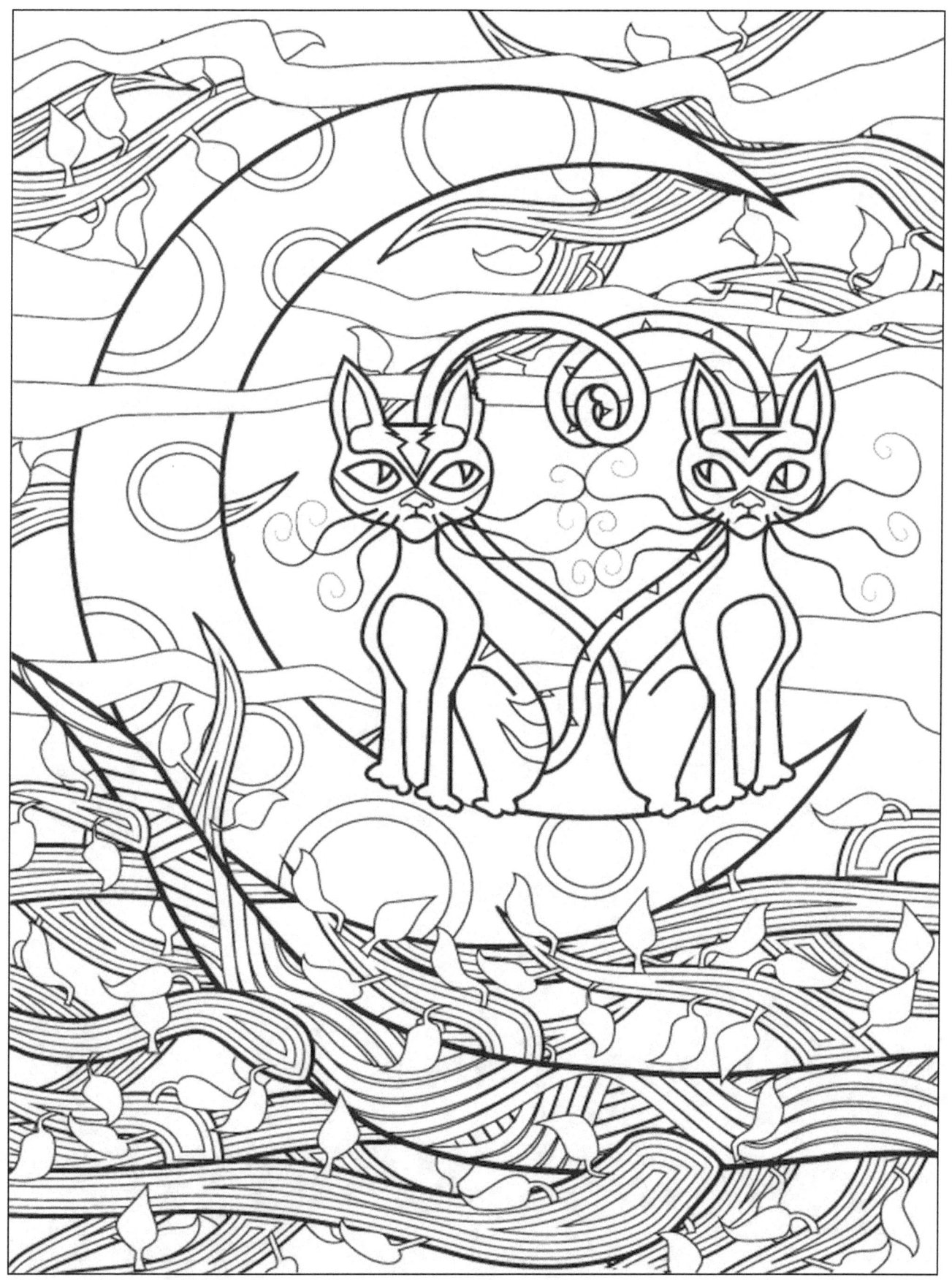

The following blank pages are for your sketching pleasure.

Thank you for purchasing this book of amazing cat designs.
I wish you serenity and enjoyment.

If you loved this adventure in stress-relieving art, please leave a **positive review.**
If you like FREE things just email me for FREE offers.

EastonEGray@gmail.com

Please look for my new collection of designs.

Peaceful moments always,

Easton E. Gray